My Spiritual Journey

Tale Of A Brazilian Immigrant: A Memoir

Maria P.S. Clark

Copyright © 2025 Maria P.S. Clark

All rights reserved. No part of this book may be reproduced or transmitted in any form or by any means without written permission from the author, except for brief quotations in reviews.

This is a work of memoir. Some names and identifying details may have been changed to protect privacy.

Printed and distributed through self-publishing platforms.

A Note from the Editor:

The family worked closely with the editors during the preparation of this book to make it easy to read—while being very careful not to "edit the Maria" out of it. So yes, you may spot a few little grammar quirks or spelling hiccups that were intentionally left right where they are. Think of them as her fingerprints on the page… or Maria giving that classic playful side-eye and saying, *"That is what I mean…"*

More than anything, we hope you can hear her voice as you read— her warmth, her humor, her heart. Even as time moves forward and life changes, these pages are here to help preserve her voice in a way that feels real and unmistakably *"Co"*. May her words bring you comfort, make you smile at the parts where she would've wanted you to, and keep Maria close in your thoughts and prayers.

Dedication

In memory and tribute to my grandmother, Clotilde Menezes Cavalcanti, (Vovo Titida) who planted the seed of faith in me, and to my brother, Dr. Antonio Alvaro Menezes de Oliveira, (Alvinho) who always believed in me, also to my daughters, Moema and Gina, to Bill, my companion through life, and to my grandchildren, the sunshine of my life, Rohwan, Asher and Riley, with love I write this story.

Epigraph

In Him who is the source of my strength I have strength for everything.

Philippians 4:13

"Our own suffering, as we learn more of Christ, touch us less than the others: most of all because there is nothing we can do but be present with them."

Rev. Edward J. Farell

Maria P.S. Clark – 1965

Just before leaving for America

Chapter 1

I have a story to tell, and I begin with the words of Charles Dickens, in A Tale of Two Cities. "It was the best of times, it was the worst of times." There is no better day to start telling a story than today,

This summer day looking at the Catalina Mountains of Tucson. I'm enjoying moments of coolness in this hot summer. The rains from the monsoon have washed the town bringing a cooling breeze down to the valley, making it a pleasant place to live. It's lovely here in Tucson when it rains on a summer afternoon.

Looking at these old and friendly heavy clouds that are still hanging around after the rain, I go back in time and space. These clouds remind me of the days of my youth in Natal, my hometown, the capital of Rio Grande do Norte in Brazil. It was a hot summer day like this one. I remember someone saying to me, "I love you so much, no one ever is going to love you more than I do. "

In Natal after the rains had come down in a pour, I used to look at nature and see everything so clean. It made me feel blessed. Many times I stood at the front window of my home smelling the rain, feeling in touch with God's creation. It made me feel happy and confident because the rain would bring new growth, new life, new hope for the farmers and to all of us. My hometown was also called the city of the sun because the sun shone most of the time, and there was never too much rain. Everybody needed the rain because we had farmland all around us, and just like here in Tucson, there was never enough rain in Natal. The people were always glad to see the rain coming and many times we went to church to pray for rain.

In these youthful days I was also waiting for life to happen to me. I knew it would come like the blessed rain. I knew I had a future and was in no hurry to know when things would start to happen. Confident and patient, I was just taking my time, enjoying the present moment, knowing that sooner or later something would happen pointing me in a direction. I had the feeling that I would live a million years or perhaps that I was even immortal. Everything bad could happen to somebody else, but not to me. I thought I was the center of the universe and everything gravitates around me. I felt invincible. I was so young and naïve. Life was wonderful and full of opportunities for me. I was in no hurry to see it happen. I was enjoying the present moment. Those were the days, the happy days of my youth: I couldn't see my selfishness and didn't know how much I had to learn. I was just young and bold.

However, I had the good fortune to have my grandma, Vovo Titida, a strong woman of great faith. She was my mentor and my model. She never told me how to live: she showed me how to live by example. She was the person who planted the seed of faith in me, and God, in his mercy, let it grow. My faith is not near as much as my grandma's. I wish I could say like the apostle Paul said, "It's not me but the Lord who lives in me." Only then I could say that I am a real Christian, one who has become like Christ. I believe this is the goal of every follower of Christ. Right now I consider myself a pilgrim on this earth.

I'm trying to follow Christ, only to find myself most of the time falling flat on my face. Sometimes I think that my falls are keeping me humble. Only for this reason, I thank God for my faults. I ask the Lord to not let me hurt my fellow companions in this pilgrimage, because I know if I do harm to anyone, I am doing harm to my Creator. I believe inside of every single person there is a divine presence. I am fortunate to have had Vovo Titida's life as an example of faith and strength.

Vovo Titida was a humble woman, yet so rich with God's grace. Now I recognize that all my life I was trying to follow in her steps. She was an honest and righteous woman, and yet she never judged anyone. She never had a negative word towards her neighbors. I remember one day, when I was a teenager, one of our friends came to visit us. This woman was criticizing a young lady who was three months pregnant and was going to get married wearing a white dress. Vovo Titida said to this friend, in front of my mother, myself and everybody who was in the room. "Naum, you must have a very short memory. Your daughter was born seven months after your wedding day, and I never saw such a well developed seven-month baby in my life." This lady said nothing to Vovo Titida, but we all felt the heaviness in the air. It was an embarrassing moment for my mother. Later on Mom told Vovo Titida, "Mother, you will kill me one of these days. I wanted to find a hole to hide in."

Vovo Titida said, "I was only refreshing her memory, and I was honest."

"You didn't need to be so honest," my mother's reply.

This was my Vovo Titida, and I was proud of her. She had a sharp tongue. She never badmouthed anyone, and never listened to injustice, she never took an insult home. Her family was wealthy. She came from a traditional political family, but she married a poor man, my grandfather. She was a widow with four children to raise and no paying job. She worked on her farm, baked cakes and sweets, and sent them to be sold in town. My mother also helped her by sewing embroideries to be sold in Natal, the capital. My mother was the oldest of the children and worked hard to help Vovo Titida. They were close friends, the best of friends.

When my mother married, Vovo Titida sold the farm to a cousin and moved in with her. Fortunately, I grew up with my Vovo Titida. I remember when I was very small, we had a nightly ritual. On our porch in the back of our home, Vovo Titida put my sisters and me inside a big tub where she bathed and changed us.

Later she took us to our beds, and there she prayed with us. She made us look up and say. "Bless us Mother in heavens, bless us Father in heavens," and then we said, "Bless us Vovo Titida."

Her response was, "God bless you all, dream with the angels." We all loved and respected her. She made me feel so safe. Later on in my life, when I was alone in a foreign country, I desperately needed her, and I only survived because of her teachings. Of this I am sure.

Some nights, sitting with Grandma on her bed, I liked to snuggle next to her enjoying a quiet time in her company. Patiently I waited for her to finish praying the Rosary. At these times she told me more stories, stories about the American soldier in Natal. Those soldiers were working at Parnamirim Base, in 1942, during World War II. She told me about the Brazilian girls who had married American soldiers. They left for America and never returned to visit their families. I wondered why they had never returned to visit their families. How could someone leave Natal and never come back? I thought to myself, I always would be back. I don't know why, but I became melancholy. It was as if somehow I knew, or like if something inside was telling me that someday I, too, was going to live in America. I couldn't comprehend my feelings. I felt as if I was missing home already, and yet I was at home. It was a weird feeling.

Other times Grandma told me stories in our backyard. My backyard was a wonderful place, a place full of wonders. It had banana trees, a big Caja tree that produced a delicious little yellow fruit, native of the Atlantic forest, avocado, papaya, guava, coconut palm, grapes, and star fruit trees. Under these trees I played with my sisters and friends from my neighborhood. The backyard was our magic place, but it wasn't planned like the backyards of today. It had an old chicken coop with a broken door and a few chickens inside, maybe six or eight with an old rooster. The rooster was king of the hill, and lived happily within his harem. This rooster liked to sing early in the morning, and also in the middle of the day, when he sang to his heart's content. For me it was the most soothing sound. I loved to hear the rooster crowing in the morning and at noon. In the morning when he woke me up, I stayed in bed for a few minutes longer, just hoping for him to crow again. That rooster had a strong, loud voice, but to me it sounded like music.

Sometimes I went alone into the backyard. I was looking for a place where I could enjoy peace and quiet, to be able to study, but I often caught myself listening to the song of the birds on the trees or simply losing myself following the trail of the red ants, and forgetting the reason why I had gone there in the first place. I also remember the happy times when I found an egg or two, inside the old chicken coop. Oh wonderful moments when a child holds in her hands the mystery of life. Only at these times I didn't realize it yet. Finding an egg inside the chicken coop was one of my magic moments, it was grand! But finding a hen's nest outside the coop, it was great excitement! It was great news; it was like finding a gold treasure. One day, when I found my nest, everybody envied me. I carried my proud self all day long, feeling like a great accomplished adventurer. It happened when I was walking, and looking around at the end of the backyard. I found a hen's nest with eight eggs in it. It was a glorious moment. I couldn't believe my great luck. I put all the eggs in an old basket, and went around showing it to my friends. Telling them of my good luck and exaggerating my tale a little bit at every stop, making sure that every kid in the neighborhood was envious of me.

Grandma also planted potatoes, corn and grapes, but a person could find everything else growing in the end of our backyard. Vovo Titida said it was because the soil was very good. We also had banana trees growing in all directions. One day grandma told me a little story. "Do you see this banana tree? It will give fine fruits and then it will die, but this other one over there, it's a better banana tree, it already has many little trees sprouting from its trunk. It's the same with people, good people will have children, yielding good fruits."

I turned around and said to her, "Vovo Titida, I will be like this old banana tree, I also will have many children. "She laughed, listening to every word that I said. My grandma always listened to what I said to her; it could be any silly little thing.

Even today I have these magical memories safe in a special little place inside me, giving me strength. When sometimes I feel hurt by the ugliness of other people's actions, I know that I'm loved. My grandmother's love is with me forever, and also with me are the memories of my backyard. It was my safe heaven then, and still is my safe place now. It will be with me forever. Even today when I'm feeling unloved, I run to my old backyard, and I find it there in my memory, just like it was yesterday. Remembering how much I was loved by my Vovo Titida, and how much I loved her, is a shield of love that covers me like magic, healing all my wounds. Thanks be to God, my foundation was love, and today I say like the psalmist said, "The banner over my head is love."

Years later, living in Tucson, Arizona, I tried to create a special place for my two daughters because I knew how important my backyard was for my emotional stability as an adult. I planted trees for my daughters: peaches, oranges, and plums. I couldn't have chickens or roosters, but I had dogs, cats, bunnies, turtles, guinea pigs, and hamsters.

One early morning I heard my daughter eight-year-old Moema screaming in the backyard, I ran to the backyard, almost having a heart attack, and there I found her favorite bunny decapitated by one of our dogs. The dog had the bunny's head into its mouth, and the body was lying on the ground. Greek tragedy big style, despite that bad experience; Moema has wonderful memories of our backyard. There were times when we camped in our backyard, and we slept together in a big tent. Inside the tent, we had a nice foam pad, making our sleeping bags as comfortable as our own beds. There were birthday parties with Mexican Piñatas and slumber parties. We also had birthdays with pool parties. One year all the second graders from Van Horn Grammar School came with their teacher, Mrs. Dee Summers, to a pool party. There were plenty of hot dogs, potato chips, and Kool-Aid for refreshment. The parties were simple, but it was lots of fun. I knew that I was making magic moments for my daughters too. Unfortunately, they didn't have a grandmother like mine, nor any other relatives close by because they were living in Brazil. I knew how important and necessary these parties would be for them later on in life.

However, in the wheel of life, things repeat themselves, and now I'm the Vovo, and my grandchildren have uncles, aunts and cousins here in the United States, most of them living close by. I love to see how happy they are playing in our backyard. Today I have only Bambina, my old cat, but my grandchildren are bringing their pets, and I end up having dogs, cats, bunnies and guinea pigs, just like when their mothers were children.

We are all so very rich, the only thing that we are lacking is lots of money. But like Vovo Titida used to say, nobody is poor, poor is the devil, because he can't have love. We are all rich by the grace of God. From a very young age, my grandma taught me that justice should be for all people, but unfortunately here on earth, it wasn't, and for this reason she only trusted God's justice. She often said that God hears the cry of the poor, the cry for justice and for life with dignity because they were His beloved. She believed that God has given us a great gift, from birth He has made us free and saved us with His holy blood.

Later on studying American history, I found out that the American Constitution has endorsed this basic law, all men are born free. Vovo Titida told me stories about the American soldiers who had fought for this freedom in Natal. They had fought Hitler's madness in my hometown in 1942. For these reasons, America became for me the land of the brave and of the free. I made up my mind that I had to come to America some day. I was aware that not too long ago the black shadow of slavery was over North and South America, it was denying the freedom of another human being. Especially in Brazil, where the slave trade was kept illegal for so long. Thanks to God, this shameful past is gone, and every human being in America has freedom guaranteed by the law of the land.

Courageous people like Rosa Parks and President L. Johnson, had successfully worked towards this feat. Rosa Parks did it for her race, President Johnson did it for his political ambitions. Nevertheless freedom and opportunity for all people was expected. America became the land of opportunity, my dreamland. The place where anyone could become successful. I was going to be there someday. I wanted to be part of the last frontier, the frontier of the mind. Someday I will be studying at an American University. I would get my degree. In my daydreams I saw myself studying in an American University. I never thought it was a crazy dream; it was hope, and I knew that hope could become a reality. I always saw myself holding my degree from an American University. At times I imagined living in America, only now I have a name for this; I was visualizing my future and I didn't know it at that time. Many times my grandma had said to me, "wanting has power." But I wasn't aware of this inner power yet, nor had I knowledge of the word visualization.

When Vovo Titida told me the stories about American soldiers in Natal, she said that in the 1940s, the propaganda in Brazil was positive towards the United States. The Americans were in Natal fighting the African campaign against the German dictator, Adolf Hitler, and our people looked at the American soldiers as heroes.

The people saw them as defenders of human freedom. They were staying at Parnamirim Field, their base in Natal, and from there they were flying straight to Africa. Grandma learned through newspapers, radio and magazines, about the agreement between the American president, Mr. Roosevelt, and our Brazilian president, the dictator, Getulio Vargas. The Brazilian President G. Vargas, let the Americans have a military base in Natal, in exchange for American technology and financial help.

In April 1941, the first project started, and in January 1942, the construction of the American base began. Vovo Titida said it was the biggest American base outside US territory. Natal in 1943 had 40,000 inhabitants, plus 15,000 American soldiers who were living on base. The Brazilians used to call it The Field "O Campo" in Portuguese. There were bombers, hydroplanes, and cargo planes. There were many B-25s flying over town. The hydroplanes were landing on the Potengy River, next to our home, delighting the neighborhood kids. At night the population was advised to keep their lights dimmed at home using black out curtains. The people obeyed because they were afraid of a surprise German attack. Natal was the closest point in South America to Senegal, Africa. From its city Dakar, the French had a steady plane delivering mail from Dakar to Natal. Its pilot was the famous writer Antoine Exupery. The Americans had a strong military campaign going on against Hitler. For this reason Natal was strategically vital to the Americans during World War II.

Grandma told me that, few bodies of American soldiers were brought from Africa to Parnamirim Base, to be sent home for burial. It was a sad thing for someone to see. Bodies of young American soldiers inside bags to be sent home to their parents. Vovo Titida said that in war there are no winners, and she felt terrible for the parents of these young soldiers. It was a great sacrifice and a high price to be paid for freedom.

Parnamirim Base was well built; even now it is still in good working condition. Many local young men worked at Parnamirim Field. My uncle Joao worked there. Brazilian mechanics and engineers helped repair the American planes with the supervision of American officers. My mother also remembered when the American President, Mr. Roosevelt, came to Natal with his wife Eleanor Roosevelt. Mom told me it was the event of the year. Many people came from Rio de Janeiro to Natal, to honor the couple as if they were royalty. For Brazil's progress in technology and in finances, the support from the American government was vital. Parnamirim Base proved to be an excellent trade. For the Brazilian people, the Americans were our heroes and powerful friends. It was only in the 1960's that the students at the universities in Brazil, were calling the Americans, imperialists and considering them the police of the world. It was with the Vietnam War that university students became critical of American foreign policies, and I was one among them.

***

However, grandma's strength came from her faith in God. Her God wasn't a distant God. Throughout my childhood I heard Grandma and my mother praising the Lord in our kitchen. When cooking or helping my Mom. Grandma would say, "Praise be to God, our Lord Jesus Christ. "My mother would answer," Forever be He praised." They were two people in love with the same loving God, peacefully working and praising Him in the same note, in the same frequency. I now believe that our kitchen was holy ground. When I was growing up, God was always a constant presence in our lives. Our God was like our daily bread. He was essential, and necessary for us to live, as the air that we were breathing. He was real; He was a God of miracles. He was a daddy, someone very close to reach. To me my God was mother and father. I believe I felt that way because I never had been close to my father. Every night we went to bed with the assurance that God was our Daddy and Mary, Jesus' mother, was our Mommy in heaven. They were protecting us, and this assurance gave us the feeling of being loved. Every night my sisters and I fell asleep peacefully. I believe it also helped us to grow up and become well-adjusted adults. Every night the routine was the same, shower, snacks, listening to Grandma stories, and prayers following with the assurance of God's protection. Our dreams were peaceful ones. Those were the days of my childhood until the day that I could understand the ugly, dirty and inexplicable behavior of our father.

Unfortunately not everything was perfect in my home as it looked. Grandma used to spend some time with her sister, who lived in another town. When she was away, we had to stay with our nanny, a witch named Lourdes, whom we called Luda. Luda saw to putting us to bed. I was lucky that at an early age, I slept in grandma's bedroom, but my two sisters had to share one bedroom and Luda was the one tucking them in bed. I will tell more about Luda later, she was also our nightmare.

In those early days of our childhood, we knew that God was a merciful God because of grandma, she was a flame of faith. It was from grandma's flame that the sparkle of faith was ignited on us. Years later, I read what Pope John XXIII had written, "Every believer in this world must become a spark of divine light." I smile with gratitude to my God, for giving me my grandmother. Vovo Titida, who with her example and her teachings had done just that. She was a sparkle of divine light not only in our home, but also in our community. Grandma was my first theologian; she was also my teacher, confident, and bosom friend. Vovo Titida taught me about the immeasurable love of Jesus for us. Growing up, I created a private Jesus for me. He was totally mine, and yet I knew that He could be totally Jesus for somebody else. However, my Jesus was quite unique. Nobody could know the Jesus that I knew, and only

Him could know the true me. I became very comfortable with my Jesus. Through grandma's stories about Him, Jesus became our trustful friend. He was someone who would never disappoint us. At an early age, I became devoted to the sacred Heart of Jesus. It still is with me today.

Every night we had to pray the rosary with our mother and grandma, thanking Jesus for his gifts for us, and for our daily bread. We also always prayed for Father to be converted. These prayers for my Father's soul only confused us more, and made us afraid of him little. Our prayers were directed to many causes, but praying for the conversion of our father and for sinners was a must. After praying the rosary Grandma told us stories about the Bible, our family or about some poetry or romance that she was reading. She always told us stories about how God was faithful for those who trusted in Him.

One of these stories was about two good friends and godfather, who were farmers and neighbors. One man told the other, "Godfather, I just finished planting my crop, and it will do good this year with the help of a good rain."

But the other man said, "Well, I just finished planting my crops too, and with God's help, I will have a good crop."

Then the first man replied, "With the help of a good rain godfather, with a good rain." The rain came and it rained little on the crops of the man who trusted on the rain, but it rained really well on the crop of the man who had put his trust on the Lord. The man with faith had the best result. We heard the story and learned that the Lord was Almighty and powerful.

Grandma also enjoyed telling us when she was young and pretty, when her family was wealthy, and her cousin Joao Villarim, was vice governor in Belem do Para, on the Amazonia. It was when rubber in Brazil was as valuable as gold, and the grand opera house was built in Belem. An entire Italian opera company came to perform. Grandma's aunt Cecilia, the vice governor's mother, had the best of things coming from Europe. Yaya, her daughter, used to say to grandma that her future husband was safe inside her father's vault. Grandma was the poor cousin; she had married my grandfather, a poor farmer. Their wealth was five children and an old farm. My mother was the oldest. They were happy living between the farm and the little town Arez, where I was born. They were there many times, for political parties. Unfortunately, my grandfather Jose, also a Portuguese, died at thirty-five years of age, from Tuberculosis. A killing disease at that time. They said he caught it in Belem, capital of Para, next to the Amazon river. In Belem grandma had part of her family involved in politics. Our rich, proud and elegant cousin Yaya Villarim, never married. Now I believe she was inebriated with her brother, Joao Villarin's power and prestige.

 I still remember cousin Yaya coming for dinner or lunch at our house. She was tall, well dressed, and very elegant. She walked like a queen. In Yaya's honor, my mother dressed us in our best clothes. The table was set with the best China. After every dinner party, showing her fingers, Yaya would renew her promises. After her death, each of us will have a diamond ring. Behind her back, my father, laughing, said, "Girls, don't wait for these diamond rings standing up, you will be tired." My mother didn't care about the promise of the rings because she knew my dad was right. Yaya had a nephew who was now in charge of the family (Salinas) Salt works refineries. Mom felt sorry for cousin Yaya, who was a lonely old woman too attached to her past and her earthly possessions. Besides, she was part of our family, and it was the right thing to do, inviting her to our home. So the dinner parties for cousin Yaya continued until the day the good Lord called her home.

What else I remember about cousin Yaya was not too nice. I remember a cruel thing I used to say about cousin Yaya. Every time I thought one of my sisters was acting selfish, I yelled, "Cousin Yaya, Yaya Villarim, you are as selfish as she is. "None of us wanted to be called cousin Yaya, it became an insult among us. For us she was our rich, refined, and selfish old cousin, but for our grandma Titida, she was her lonely cousin, without children or grandchildren, and very poor because all she had was money. Grandma also used to say, "Money is my slave, I'm not the slave of money."

It wasn't nice that we judged cousin Yaya, calling her selfish. For this unkind behavior towards cousin Yaya, now I ask for her forgiveness, because today I also believe, as my grandma Titida did, that Yaya was a poor and lonely old soul. However, she was also a great lady, she had class, and I admired her hair-do, jewelry, clothes and airs of royalty. The way she looked and carried herself was unique as well as the way she talked: she never raised her voice. When cousin Yaya was talking to grandma, I used to listen, only to soon become bored and lose interest; her conversations were a long line of complaints. Thanks to this classy lady, very early in my life I realized that money was not much, it was just a tool that we need in this life. Because of cousin Yaya, I associated happiness with inner wealth not money. But who knows, cousin Yaya, for sure must have had her virtues, perhaps they were just unknown to us. She wasn't a mean person, she was just an eccentric. She was more like a ghost, coming from the past, living in her own peculiar way. Sometimes I believed that her only touch with reality and entertainment was at our home when she was invited for lunch or dinner. Nobody else invited her. When cousin Yaya passed away, we found out that her only nephew inherited all her treasures. The statue of the Venus of Milo, representing Aphrodite. I still remember that it had come from Italy and was always in her living room. It was so beautiful! The glassed eyes were expressive; they looked as if they were real. Today I wonder if this statue still exists, it was one of the wonders of my childhood. Later on my father bought a statue of Venus from Italy, his pride and joy, but not similar to cousin's Yaya. This precious statue, my sister Fatima and I broke in a fight. We sweat it all day long waiting for our father to come home, my mother telling us, wait girls until your father finds out. When he came home, my sister and I were the best friend holding our hands together, waiting for our faith. However, my mother told a white lie, she said to him it was her who accidently broke the statue.

Backing track, remembering my sweet unforgettable grandma. Titida was in love with life. She romanced life. Life for her was a great gift from the Lord, and with every sunshine, a new and great adventure could be waiting for her. "God be praised for the freshness of this new day, God be praised for the song of the birds." She said this with all her heart, meaning every word. She was always ready to face a new day. She marveled at every flower, every fruit tree, every butterfly, at everything coming from nature. Sometimes looking at our young brother, Alvinho sleeping, she said, "Blessed are those who have the peace of a sleeping child in their hearts, they are truly blessed." For my grandma Titida, every birth was a miracle, every child a gift from above. She loved the moon, the sun, the beach, and the wind. She taught us to see the breath of the Holy Spirit in the wind. This is the reason why I love the wind so much. I love feeling the morning breeze on my face, and it is because in my subconscious mind, I keep saying, "The wind brings the Holy Spirit". Every night she reminded us of the power and glory of the Lord, and gave thanks for the gift of the Holy Spirit, the gift of life. Morning and night. She praised God. He was the love of her life.

Today I made this prayer mine, trying to follow into her shoes. I also say, "God be praised for the freshness of the morning, and for this new day." I give the Lord my thanks and praise, in the same way that she did it. For me the best way to face the day is elevating my soul to our creator. There is nothing better than starting a new day happy and with confidence in our Lord the Father, Son and Holy Spirit. When I asked grandma Titida if there were three gods, she answered, "No, not three gods, it's only one God, one creator, but there are three holy persons in one." Wanting her to explain it better to me, she said, "Do you see this apple? God is like this apple. An apple has the skin, the meat and the core; there are three parts, but it is one apple. God is three in one, just like an apple. Accepting her reasoning, I said, "Oh! I understand grandma" This was the end of our conversation because for me, she had explained well the mystery of the Holy Trinity, in her great pragmatic ways. My grandma was my white guardian angel and my nanny Luda, the dark one.

    Science was not Grandma's strong subject. She had only a vague knowledge about Galileo's work, and the theory of relativity wasn't her favorite subject, but all that she had to know was that the universe was immeasurable, and only an Almighty God could have created such a wonder. She told me that comparing mankind with the size of the universe, we were like little ants. Yet a powerful God had made us His image. He gave us a soul, a spirit like his, and with great humility, He came down and was crucified, for love of us, making us His children. Sometimes I wonder why God asked this sacrifice from his Son? What tremendous mystery love holds. It's too profound for my mind. Nowadays scientists are finding that besides the theory of relativity, the universe is still expanding, because of a creative force that they are calling, "dark matter and dark energy". Such discoveries, they can't explain very well, they just know that it exists, and it is a creative force, somehow inexplicable so far. Why did God create us in his image? We are so insignificant, so small, why us? I can only come out with one explanation, it is because besides being an Almighty creator, He is also humble, and out of His great humility and love, He created us in His image. Grandma Titida was right when she taught me that God was humble, and in front of such great humility and love, I cry with gratitude. I don't need to study theology, to learn how to love my God. And I pray for the gift of faith, for His peace and humility. I ask for these graces and for the privilege to follow Jesus, all the days of my life. I trust that the Lord is not going to look at my faults because of His love and mercy for us sinners. I hope that someday, reflecting his bright light on me, He is going to be blinded by his own love, and I will be embraced by Him, and we will become one. This will happen without my merits.

I believe, the Lord Jesus himself, gave all the joy that was inside Vovo Titida's heart. Nothing could destroy her joy. She never lost her faith in Divine Providence. One day she told me, "Co, (my nickname, she always called me, Co) remember that the good times come and go away, but when bad times come, remember, they too go away. Nothing stays the same, and the only thing that doesn't change is change itself. Maybe heaven won't have a measurement of time, because heaven is forever, but everything here on earth changes. Whether we like it or not. Everything changes with time, or time will change everything."

Grandma was happy and strong, because the Lord was her fortress, her happiness, her strong hold. I pray for this strength, replacing my anxiety with joy of a pure heart, a trustful heart.

Grandma also adored literature. William Shakespeare and Victor Hugo were among her favorite authors, but she told me that she always loved a good story. It didn't matter who had written it. She was a simple, smart woman, who loved to read. She loved to tell us about the Crusades, about the French king, Charles Magnus' victories against the Arabs.

We were delighted with these stories. Many nights, with our bedroom window open, looking throughout the sky, I dreamed with open eyes. When the nights were dark, the sky was more like a tapestry of stars above us. Looking at the Southern Cross, I felt part of this vast universe, and part of the Crusades. I lived in the magic world created by my grandmother's imagination.

    Grandma Titida was the school teacher, the doctor and the healer in our farm. She prescribed regular medicine and healing herbs for the people at the farm and at the nearby city of Arez, the small town where I was born and where we had our family roots. People also believed in her influence with the Lord, they believe she had a direct line with heavens. Many people asked for her prayers, especially pregnant women. I guess people had good results through her prayers. I never really asked why everybody wanted her to pray for them. To me she was wonderful, I loved her, but I never thought of her as a saint, not with her temperament. She had a strong personality, and she could be very angry at times. I remember a story she told me about her brother, who was the Mayor of Ares, a city where she had two houses. One day her brother, uncle Conrad, asked her to rent the larger home to the city, it was spacious, and would be perfect to become City Hall. However, after three years he had never paid rent, she asked him many times for the rent and always gave her an excuse. One day she decided to go to Natal, the capital of my state, and asked for an audience with the governor. ne never doubted her love for me, but she never spared the rod, and if I did something wrong and needed discipline, she was the first one to discipline me. I could take all the scolding from her, but I was mortified if my father gave me a stern look. Grandma Titida taught elementary school for the children living on the farm. She was teaching us all the time with her stories and by her example.

    On one occasion one of her godsons came to ask for her advice. He told her that he was afraid to accept a new job. She asked him why. He told her that it was because he knew nothing about the job.

She told him that nobody was born knowing anything, but the good Lord had given everybody a brain, with the capacity to learn. She told him to go on and accept the job, and not let fear cripple him. This was an unforgettable lesson that I learned from her.

Later on in my life when I came to the United States, I knew very little English, but I told my husband that I was going to find a job. I didn't understand American culture, language or money, and yet I applied at a local bank for a job as a teller, and I got the position. When I told my husband that I was going to work as a bank teller, he laughed and said that the people who had hired me were crazy because I didn't know how to make change for a dollar. He told me, "Don't tell anybody which bank you are working for. "I became angry with him and told him that he was right, I didn't know but I was going to learn. I believed in myself because my grandma Titida had said, "Nobody is born knowing anything, but we can learn." The reason why the person in personnel hired me was because I had an unofficial translation of all my papers from college. I had brought it with me, thinking that perhaps it could be helpful to me. The person who was doing the hiring interviews seemed impressed and hired me on the spot.

Grandma Titida told me many times that a nation that doesn't protect its unborn children and doesn't respect its elders, will be doomed. Abortion is an ugly sin, and from whom will the young people learn, if not from their elders? I often wonder what she would think of today's societies, with care homes for the elders and legalized abortion? When I hear the media talking about one of these topics, I think about my grandmother, turning in her grave. She believed families should take care of their own, and as for abortion, she did abhor the thought of it. Because of her, I, too, detest this unspeakable sin.

Grandma Titida never worried about money or the lack of it. When I asked her if we were rich or poor, she told me that we were rich by the grace of God, poor was the devil, because he couldn't love. When in need, I should trust Divine Providence, and all would work out for the best. She had the peace of the Lord in her heart. I always felt so good and protected next to her. I never saw her anxious or too preoccupied with anything. She raised all her children on the farm, working hard, selling her embroideries, cakes and sweets, as her whole income she did the best she could cutting down some trees and selling wood. With help from Divine Providence and hard work, she raised and educated her children. Her favorite passage from the apostle Paul was, "Dismiss all anxiety from your minds. Present your needs to God in every form of prayers in a petition full of gratitude. Then God's own peace, which is beyond understanding, will stand guard over your hearts and minds, in Christ Jesus."

This prayer became mine when my younger brother Alvinho, was dying with AIDS. Now at any difficult times in my life I rely on it. Thanks to God, grandma had healthy children, nor did she have any serious illness. The only doctor who went to the farm was the veterinarian. She was the doctor for her family and for the people on the farm. I can imagine how hard she had to work to survive without a husband and without a steady income. I believe it was Divine Providence who took care of her. Grandma knew a lot about herbs, she prescribed herbal tea for many illnesses.

Many were the roles of my grandma in the community. She was always busy, multitasking and the more she gave of herself, the more she received from the Lord. She was a very wealthy lady, with the grace of God. Sometimes at bed time I would find her praying, then I asked her, "Vovo Titida, aren't you tired, you baked a lot today are you still praying? Aren't you afraid of dying? "And her answer to me was, "I'd rather die because I'm tired than because I'm doing nothing. If I do nothing I will die much faster because I will die with rusty bones. "She told me once that one of the worst pain in life was hunger pain. For this reason she was always helping the less privileged.

She told me that her sister, aunt Sinha Louisa. (Sinha, was a name given to women who owned slaves)Aunt Louisa, had many real estate properties in Natal. I remember going with my grandmother to visit one of her friends in the best part of Natal, grandma telling me that many houses on that street belong to great aunt Sinha Louisa.

When she told grandma that she was going to request it all to the Catholic Church, Grandma, who was taking care of her, because she was terminally ill, had said to her, "Sinha Louisa, these are your properties, you can give it to whomever you want. "My aunt donated all her real estate to the church, and Grandma took care of her until the end of her life. This was one important lesson that I learned from my Vovo: family ties were more important than material gains. She helped her sister out of love. Remembering her teachings, when I had my children I told them, 'what is important is inside us, we can't see it with our eyes, we can only feel it." Vovo's own words.

I didn't only teach my children this truth, but also my students when I taught middle school in the heart of South Tucson, the poorest area of town. I used to stop my class five minutes before the bell rang and talk with my students asking them about their family life. Once in a while I asked them, "What can we buy at the Shopping Mall? Can we buy love, hugs and kisses, peace, health, family, friends? "Their answer was, "No Miss, we can't." Then the Mall isn't that important to us. We need some things from the mall, but they can't make us happy. Once in a while some student would say, "But Miss we need stuff, everybody wants nice things. "And I would reply, "Yes we do, but they aren't the most important things in life, just remember what I said."

My poor students often didn't have the basic necessary things in life. I used to visit some of them at their home, mostly the troublemakers. After school, I made some home visits with my colleague Mary, another teacher who had the same students in her math class. Some days it was around supper time, when we stopped at their homes. We were always welcome, but the kids knew they were in trouble. It was a surprise visit that for sure they didn't expect. I saw that these students were living in small, old and filthy trailers. Making these visits we saw a tremendous amount of poverty. These visits helped me see the whole picture. I saw the total reality of the life of my students and it made all the difference. These home visits made it easier for me to make a bridge between my class and the community. Sometimes we saw what they were having for supper, and coming back home it was hard for me to eat my own supper. Sometimes I was swallowing my tears with the food. These families were mostly families of illegal immigrants, these people thought they couldn't apply for food stamps. Some families had three and four children. At this time I saw and touched Lady Poverty, and I didn't like it, because I remembered Grandma saying that hunger hurts. I was frustrated because I thought I wasn't doing enough. I tried to help, reporting some situations to the school counselors or to the psychologist. I learned one thing from these home visits, when I saw a human being in need, I didn't ask about papers; all I wanted to do was find a way to help. I could see myself reflected in their eyes and realized that we were made of the same material. I could see the reason why some of these kids were misbehaving in class. These home visits helped my students and myself tremendously. I realized these days that I had brought my grandma into my classes, because my words were her words, once said to me. Her spirit was alive; her teachings were forever inside me.

    Years before I had resented the undocumented people because when my younger brother Alvinho came here to study English for a year, my mother had to pay $4000 to District One school for one semester. I was paying my taxes but the law didn't allow my brother to study for free. The superintendent of District One, in Tucson, told my husband and I that we had to pay for my brother. For this reason the system seems unfair to us. However, life sometimes is ironic. Years later I was teaching undocumented children at the same school district, and teaching them with love. Today I thank the Lord for giving me the opportunity to teach at Apollo Middle School and Sunnyside high, in the South side of Tucson because it made me more compassionate. I understood that in life things can't be all black or white. We need to act with mind and heart.

I was thirteen years old and still praying the nightly rosary with Grandma. Part of her audience was mom, my sisters Fatima, Eneida, me, and my brother Bosco who was five years old., we could hardly wait for the end of the last Hail Mary to run and play outside. For us, the Rosary seemed endless. Sometimes grandma asked me, "Do you have ants in your pants"? We girls were not allowed to go outside and play at night on our street. After the rosary we begged our mother to go and sometimes she allowed us. Most times we stayed inside getting ready to shower, have a snack before going to bed.

Some nights when the moon was big and full in the sky, Grandma told stories that were part of our folklore. There was this story about bad women, those who had tempted and disrespected holy priests. (At this time in our home priests were considered holy, priests with bad behavior were unknown to us. Some of these tales were blaming women for their behavior. In the Northeast of Brazil, our society was and still is a macho society. One of these stories was "The mule without a head". Some young women, who had tempted parish priests, and those who were having affairs with priests, for punishment for their ugly sin, had become mules without heads the nights when the moon was full. God allowed them to become these mules without heads, just like the werewolves. At night from the strength of the full moon, people could see these mules without heads galloping all night through the fields; running without peace, trying to find their heads. Some people swore they had seen them. My sisters and I were scared to death of the mule without a head. It was with great respect that we kissed the hands of our friendly priests when some of them came to our home for lunch. Today I laugh remembering these stories.

Grandma taught me a lot with her example, however, her stories were powerful ones, and we all believed them whole-heartedly. Later on we did separate the folklore from reality. Now I know how lucky I am because I had a wonderful fairy godmother. She was for me the salt of the earth, the salt of my life. I wish I had a faith like hers. Today, in a good way, I am envious of her tranquility, of her lack of anxiety. I need to be more like she was, relying and trusting completely on Divine Providence. I wish the good Lord had given me the same faith. If today, someone would ask me what belief I hold, I would say that I still hold on to my faith: my Catholic faith, and God willing I will die a Roman Catholic. It was planted in me by my grandma, Vovo Titida. I absorbed it into my soul and mind. It took over my entire being, and without my faith, I am nothing. I could be like a boat without direction on an open sea. I can't separate it from my soul, mind and body because every molecule in me needs my faith. My faith is God breathing in me. God is my breath, the breath of life. Today I realize that my church is in poor shape, however, I believe it will not sink, God is in charge. My faith doesn't make me a saint. I remember Grandma telling me that the devil also believes. I'm far from becoming a saint or a holy person. If I had nothing else impeding me from becoming a holy woman, it would be my temperament that would stop me. I want to believe that I inherited it from someone else in my family. People close to me know that when I lose my temper, I become a hurricane in fury, and I'm not proud of it. Many times I have tried to control it, and many times I have failed. But I also have one quality; I'm humble enough to ask for forgiveness. It's hard and embarrassing to acknowledge this fault, but out of honesty I have to admit. I believe that God is still among us, despite all our faults. God worked miracles in my grandma's life, and today He also has shown His mercy, for a poor sinner like me. He is a father and mother. Nothing can stop God's love for us. Enemy of souls must be a jealous creature, because he can't stop God's eternal love for his creation. We are under the banner of love. The love of a powerful Almighty God. This thought helps me at night, when putting my head on my pillow, I sleep in peace, the sleep of a trusting child. I believe that all churches, worshiping God, are good. Like the Italians who say that all roads lead to Rome, it's also true that all churches pave the way to heaven. However, my truth is that the Catholic Church is the universal church. Jesus, the son of the living God, is the head of this church, but I also believe that in heaven, paradise or nirvana, I will find many Jews, Muslims, Protestants, and people of all faiths, because what is impossible for us to understand, isn't impossible to God. And who am I to understand God's plan for us humans? God is mystery and so are we, his people. We are mystical people, surrounded by mysteries. No human mind can comprehend God's mysteries unless He reveals them to us.

    I will never say that the Catholic Church is a perfect church, but it is the perfect church for me. It has lasted over two thousand years. It has made many mistakes, terrible mistakes, but this doesn't surprise me because, unfortunately, we are imperfect human beings. I hope that with every mistake we are learning. I don't put my trust in the Pope, head of the Catholic Church here on earth, but in God the Father, the Son and the Holy Spirit, the holy trinity, in heaven. Like St. Therese said, today our hand, feet and head, are the hand, feet and heads of Jesus on earth. Every human being is a walking church, the temple of the Holy Spirit. I learned this from my grandma Titida, this is the belief that I still hold on, and I always will, it's my Catholic faith. I hope that it will be the faith of my children, grandchildren and future generations.

Perhaps I reminded my grandma Titida, of herself in her youth, with the difference of the color of our skin, because she was white as snow and I was of mixed blood-brown like my father. Physically we were different, but spiritually we were kin and bosom friends. I was a romantic young lady, only sixteen years old, who loved poetry, as much as my grandma did, and like her, I loved God, nature and life. She told me that she had danced at many family balls. She had danced like no one else had at parties in her family home. She also said that she was a beautiful redhead in her youth and was never without a dance partner because of her reputation of having golden feet. I believe that this grandma of mine, also loved like nobody else ever loved, because of what she told me about her romance with a young poet named, Louis, who she affectionately called Loulou. She romanced Loulou before my grandfather, but she saved Loulou's poems as true literary treasures. She said, they were lovely and sensitive poems, too beautiful to be destroyed. When she talked about my grandpa, she said he was a generous soul, a good man, and a good husband. I compare Loulou as being Vovo's golden key that Vovo Titida lost, and my grandpa, her silver one. To me Loulou was her youth dream and grandfather her reality. I, too, was a romantic like her, and hoped that life would be a gentle mother to me, not the stepmother that it had been for my grandma.

When I asked her what had happened to Lolou poems, she told me she had given them to her sister for safe keeping. I wanted to find and read his poems. By that time my aunt Sinha Louisa, grandma's sister, had passed away, all the poems were lost: a pity.

Those were the days when my world was colorful and I was madly in love with life and everything around me. I was happy because I felt truly alive. I knew that I was part of nature, part of God's plan and fit so well into life's puzzle, I had so many dreams waiting to happen. Life started happening, and day by day it slowly developed showing my path, sometimes showing two roads to choose.

When I was sixteen and in love for the first time, my grandma always defended my boyfriend's serenades in front of my father, or as my attorney, defending me from one thing or the other. Usually after a night of serenade, my father got up from bed angry as a bear. He said that people should respect his right to have a good night's sleep. He had important work to do in the morning. Some vagabond had the audacity to play guitar under his bedroom window all night long. We all knew that father was exaggerating, the serenade only lasted one hour or so. At his comments, I made myself very small, and tried to disappear from his sight. My mother kept very quiet but Grandma spoke her mind. She was the only one in our home who wasn't afraid of my father. She told him that she had enjoyed the serenade and that the music was beautiful. The music was soothing to her soul, and it had helped her go back to sleep. She slept soundly until morning. My father wouldn't say another word after her comments. For some unknown reason Father always avoided confrontation with her.

My eighteen-year-old boyfriend, who was in my class at Atheneu preparatory school, did not like school. He also worked at a local radio station. For me this was the glory. I thought he was a celebrity. Today I realize he was only a young boy handling an insignificant little job, helping with the records. His job was to make sure all the records were ready for the radio's programs, later he worked with the controls. However, I was so proud to say that my boyfriend worked at the local radio station and I bragged about it to all my friends. They also thought it was marvelous because none of us had a job. In our culture our parents took care of our financial needs; only after college did we have to find a job. It was a law for middle class people.

Remembering my first kiss today, I will try to tell when, where and how it did happen. My boyfriend I was 16 years old and I was 14, not allowed to date. But love finds a way. It was in December, a gentle breeze was blowing from the beach. A strong aroma of jasmine was in the air. I told my parents I needed to go to church. The people in my small town were praying a novena asking for rain, and I was going to join them. With everybody's approval and delight, I left home with the complicity of my rosary, and the moon, because it was a very dark night.

That night I not only went to meet my boyfriend behind the church, but I received my first unforgettable kiss. The kiss was so very gentle. He hardly touched my lips. However, it had the sweetness of honey and gave me the sensation of heaven. I felt that the moment was eternal. It was special and magical. I could never feel that same way ever again and I never did. Now I understand, it had the taste of innocence.

At that time, the entire universe was mine. At that moment I had heavens and earth under my feet. Oh! the tenderness of that first kiss. It was a genuine romance. I felt my heart singing and thought that with me the angels in the heavens were singing too. I just had hit heaven. Sweet memories of a distant past. It was December, summer of 1958.

My boyfriend was also very generous. With his first paycheck he bought a pearl necklace for me on my sixteenth birthday. Later I found out it cost him all of his paycheck. He was my first boyfriend and I was his first girlfriend, we were passionately in love with each other. I believed everyone else could see our love through our eyes. We were young and naïve but our love was pure and platonic. This lover of mine was also a bohemian who played the guitar like an angel but didn't like to study, especially history, one of my favorite subjects. I believe at that time his passion was his guitar and me. Nothing else was important to him. But school was important to me. I had set my goal to become an attorney because it was never my intention to be supported by a husband and Law was my passion, it was in our blood. I guess college kept us apart and the magic broke. Soon he married someone else and I realized my castle was made of sand, my dreams with him, the ocean waves took away. Today he is an old man, his wife supported him all their lives. I am glad he is a happy married man. Life showed he could not be the right fellow for me. I wasn't the woman who could make him happy. No man was born to become my boss. He was no exception, like all the men from my area in Brazil, were the feudal Lord of their wives. Because my boyfriend and I focused only on our puppy love, I couldn't see how different we were from each other. Only much later did I understand the depth of these differences.

Unfortunately we were not made for each other. However, it was my first love and I wish I had told Vovo Titida about my first kiss but I never spoke with her about it. I wanted to, but I was afraid of her reaction. I thought it could be a sin or disrespectful to talk to her about it. Not even to a priest in confession because I wasn't sure it was a sin. It was so sweet, and I wanted to be kissed again but I couldn't tell a single soul where and when I was kissed, without damaging my reputation. Other times I thought it couldn't be a sin; it had made me feel so wonderful. It was such a dilemma, I couldn't understand my feelings, everything was new to me. I had no one to talk to; my sisters were too young with no boyfriends. I finally decided to tell a friend about my kiss. My friend, who was a protestant Christian told me not to worry about it, it wasn't a sin. She had kissed many boys and was sure she was going to meet me in heaven some day, because the lord Jesus had already saved us. At the time I didn't buy into this theology. I believed that we were redeemed by the cross of Jesus, but only if we were doing the right thing down here on earth. I believed we had to do our best to deserve to enter into the kingdom of God. This was my Catholic belief. Only when my hair became gray. Did I change my mentality, and began thinking that we should do good deeds for the love of God, and not to deserve paradise. My girlfriend didn't help much, I had mixed feelings about the kiss. The truth was that at sixteen, I was horny, and discovering some unknown forces inside me. I knew nothing about libido or hormones.

Thinking back about my high school years, that day had been a hot summer day, with no rain in sight, but later that night, after my kiss, when I was enjoying my boyfriend's company so much, heavy clouds suddenly came in, and we had a downpour. It rained cats and dogs. I had to run back home, and when I got home soaked, my family was so happy with the rain that nobody paid attention to me. I was afraid that just by looking at me everybody would guess what had happened. My face was an open book, and everyone could guess that something special had happened. Quickly I changed into my pajamas and went to bed. However, with my heart still beating fast, I couldn't fall asleep. I stayed in bed for a long time, in a state of grace. I wanted to tell very body that I was in love, yet reason told me to be very quiet and say nothing to anyone. It was hard to keep so much happiness inside me. Next day life was absolutely wonderful. I was in love and the whole world was smiling at me. The sky was bluer, trees were more beautiful. I felt wonderfully happy, and the earth became heaven.

My world was colorful and wonderful, and I knew life was just beginning for me. Soon I discovered the meaning of passion, and the strong chemistry between us. Like a rose bud I was slowly opening to life, and finding it mysteriously delicious. I was so naïve and ingenuous that I didn't understand my feelings or what that chemistry was. I was madly in love with life and with everything around me and was happy, because I was feeling truly alive.

My first romance lasted through my high school years. I made the painful decision to finish our relationship. It had to be done. I was going to law school and the differences were too many between us. He barely finished high school and decided to play guitar in a band. At that time my spirit was soaring high. I wanted more for myself than just a husband. Like the Brazilian poet once wrote, my love was not forever, because it was a flame, but it was infinite as it lasted. I have sweet memories of those high school years.

I thought that all I had was time, and my youth would last for long good years, maybe my moments would last forever, maybe for an eternity. Unfortunately it passed by me in a flash, too fast. Now here I am telling my story. With the wine of youth gone and my cup empty, I decided it was time to write down my experiences.

My father once told me a story about the goddess of youth who was living in the Olympus. She served her guests the wine of youth, and it was so delicious that everybody drank it too fast, only to find out later that the goddess could never refill one's cup. Just like the guests on the Olympus, I realized that I drank the wine of my youth too fast, and my cup could never be filled again. Foolish mortal, I had become inebriated with the wine of youth, like everybody else my youth was gone before me, and I thought I knew better.

Now some people may call me an old lady. But I refuse to be a senior citizen. I don't even know if I'm old. All I know is that I have lived for many years. However, In reality I'm just a happy old lady young at heart and the word old fits me just fine, because I know that my face is now showing signs of the time and the wind. There is nothing that can transform a person more rapidly than time and wind. As a matter of fact, they change just about everything.

Today if someone asks me, "What is a good life?" I will answer that a good life is a productive life. Don't think about the years and don't fear old age. As long as we are doing something to help others, we are productive. Be strong in the Lord. I don't feel old as long as I am doing some good work. My body may be slowing down but my soul is strong, and I am my soul. I'm a creative spirit waiting here for the best to come. I'm always trying to be positive because I believe the Lord is positive. Now I have two handsome grandsons, Rohwan and Asher and a very beautiful granddaughter, Riley. To watch them grow and be successful comprises many of the reasons why I want to stay on this earth a little longer. Rohwan is at the University of Arizona studying to become a Genetic engineer. Asher is still deciding what path he is going to take but whatever he choses, I am sure it will be fulfilling.

I'm writing my little story for my grandchildren, but I worry it may bore them to death, and hope that somehow I can make it interesting for them, the sunshine of my life. I also hope that my story will help their mothers understand this old Vovo a little better because my culture was so different from theirs.

My intention is not to teach, I have nothing to teach, only much to learn but I have a lifetime of experiences to share. In this attempt to tell my story I am undressing my own soul in a deeper and special way for you all to come to know me a little better. I want to tell the way it was with no half-truth, and I will show myself with my strengths and weaknesses, my virtues and my sins, with my sufferings and my joys. May the Lord bless and inspire me to write with a clear mind and a loving heart, because all that wasn't positive in my life wasn't important. It was only the pluses that really counted. Today, my hair is gray and my body is rapidly wrinkling, but my soul-this eternal mystery-is young and strong, and my heart has never wrinkled. Some days when I'm not looking at a mirror, and the aches and pains throughout my body are giving me a break, I feel twenty something all over again, and life? Oh it is good, it feels good. It's wonderful to be alive because I have inside me this vibrant and happy soul that is forever young.

Rohwan, Asher and Riley, I must tell about my young brother, your great uncle Dr. Antonio Alvaro Cavalcante Menezes de Oliveira, but for us he was our Alvinho, it was his nickname, and also for his friends and his clients, because he preferred to be called this way. When a client called him, "Dr. Alvaro," he would say, "Call me just Alvinho please." He was an attorney, however, in Brazil we call a lawyer, doctor. My father was also an attorney, my cousin who lives in Sao Paulo, and myself who was in Law school.

Alvinho's story is also mine because he was the love of my life, the salt of the earth. His short life here on earth was all about love and suffering, joy and sadness. He loved and lived life intensely. He was a vibrant young man who became a successful lawyer, and nothing in his life indicated that later on he would have a tragic end, a tragic death. His life and his death, above all his death, changed all of us in our family. We became more humble and more understanding about the terrible disease, AIDS. We become better people. Alvinho took a test to become a Judge, and passed the test. In Brazil, judges are not appointed, they must apply for the position. He decided to come to the USA before assuming his position. He told me, "I will bring mom and "Tata", my sister Fatima, to your home and I am going to travel all over the United States. I told him it was an excellent idea. However, in 1990, he came down with AIDS.

When I heard the terrible news, I flew to Natal. It was the worst trip I ever had made.

He died in 1993. He was 32 years old. It was the most terrible three years.

After Alvinho's brief passage through earth, none of us could feel or be the same. How could we handle this tragedy? How did we bear the pain of his death, how could we not despair? At the time when we were going through, we didn't know how, but now I understand that our strength came from above, because it was God, who kept us together. It was our belief that we were created from God's image and that He was real. For this reason we have the capacity to love, and we consequently suffer because we love. This is our mystery, our essence is love. This is why our hearts yearn to go back to our beginning, to the infinite love of God. Out of love the Son of God has redeemed us on a cross, and because we love, we suffer our own Calvary. Conscious or unconscious we all suffer, and are crucified with Christ. We are yearning for our God, the supreme love. This is the process, and we don't understand why. Why do we suffer and die? Why does the sun shine on the good and on the bad, just the same? Are we going to be forgiven or are we going to pay for our wrongdoing? My father used to say that purgatory was here on earth, that our Lord was merciful. He was not a religious man, however, he believed in a just God.

Many times I have asked. What is hidden beyond the Black Hole out there in the universe? What is black matter, what is black energy? Does anyone know the future of mankind or the future of planet earth? Anybody with an educated guess? Mystery is our reality, we are mystic people, we are surrounded by mysteries. Why, when looking in a dark night, when the sky is full of shining stars, our spirit desires something more, and one feels lifted up to find something bigger than the vast universe? Our spirit soars looking for the unknowing, and wanting something more and incomprehensive? Could this be our thirsting for God, our creator? It must be, because every human being yearns for God, conscientiously or not. In one of these moments one can truly say like the psalmist, "my soul thirst for God more than the earth thirsts for water." MORE ABOUT ALVINHO.

Out of love, Alvinho's death and sufferings changed us all. Because of our faith we came out of this tragedy as better people. We are now more understanding, more tolerant and less prejudiced toward many issues in this life, including the gay community. We learn through suffering to respect the differences. It was deep, very deep suffering.

My brother Alvinho thirsted for life and for love more than anybody that I knew. He was sixteen, and just like I had felt once upon a time, he felt he was the center of the universe. At this age he came to my house in Tucson to study English as a second language. He stayed with us for the whole year of 1977. I loved my baby brother Alvinho like my own son, and I did everything that I could to make him comfortable and happy here in my home. At this time he was healthy and happy, my daughter Moema was a baby, and I was pregnant with Gina, my second daughter. Our lives were good, we never had to deal with tragedy until the day when we learned about our little brother and AIDS. Even today it still sounds and feels surrealistic and absurd.

I was a teenager when Alvinho was born, my sisters and I fell instantly in love with this tiny baby, whom our father named Antonio Alvaro. Immediately we began calling him Alvinho. However, Alvinho's time in this earth was too brief. In his short lived life he grew up and became a talented and special young man, who today is an angel, among many in the city of God.

In our Christian faith we know that death is our new beginning but this knowledge doesn't help the hurt, and the profound pain when we lose a young loved one. We still miss our loved ones and hurt just the same. Alvinho was the pride and joy of our lives.

My loving little brother was the baby in our family. When he grew up he became a perfect gentleman. From an early age he showed a compassionate heart towards all human beings. He was a brilliant young man, who happened to also be born gay. In 1990 he found out that he was infected with the AIDS virus. Unfortunately he became one more victim of AIDS, one more number, one more statistic.

For the first time in our family we were hit with such tremendous tragedy, and even today, almost twenty years later, my heart still aches for my little brother. Our lives had been so good, until the day when his misfortune affected all of us, and never again did we feel the same because inside our hearts we are forever caring this terrible and painfully thorn, what is living without Alvinho.

The AIDS virus brought us shame, fear, pain, and despair. All these feelings became our daily companions, with the knowledge that our little brother was sentenced to an early death, and there was nothing that anyone could do to help. Many times together we cried asking, "Dear God why? Why is this terrible disease among us? Why this is happening to us? Why my brother? No, no, not my little brother." But there was no answer; there was no hope, just pain. We experienced profound pain, and profound love at the same time. Living under the shadow of AIDS was our daily reality, and what a terrible shadow it was the smell of death. However, our love became strong as steel. It held us together; it kept us afloat. There were times when we thought that we were sinking into the deepest despair. In these moments our faith in God saved us. We hugged him, all of us, showing him that he was loved.

I remember one day when we all thought our sister was going to lose her mind. I was at home in Natal visiting, and my sister started crying and soon became irrational. She was screaming, "No isn't true, it's a lie, he is not going to die, he is not going to die." She became hysterical, and we didn't know what to do. Finally I shook her up and told her to stop, but my mother came to us an held my sister's head, she started praying, and then I also started praying the Our Father with her. It had a calming effect on her and she stopped yelling. We were holding one another, and it seemed to be for an eternity. Fortunately we had each other and our faith to hold on to it, and that was the way we were. We couldn't heal our brother, but we could be there for him. Together, leaning on each other, feeling the desperation of hell, we survived Alvinho's Calvary and death. My Lord, the powerful force of your love, let nobody underestimate it. Today, twenty years after Alvinho's death, my grief has been transformed, but never eliminated. It will be with me as long as I live.

With the passing of time some of us become skilled and wise, and others just learn how to get by, sometimes by hanging there. I belong to this last category of ordinary people. Those who acquired some knowledge the hard way. These last old fogies have come a long way and have become tough as leather. We are living and feeling on this earth like a wrinkled and comfortable pair of leather shoes. Some day the shoes will be left behind and the souls will soar free throughout the universe. These old fogies learned to take life easy, waiting on the Lord's mercy, and wanting to impress no one but God. We have learned that life is a gift, and we learned to take it easy and enjoy it without passing judgment on no one. The sun shines on the rich and privileged but also on the poor and destitute just the same. These ordinary people at the end of their journey have only their simple life story to tell. Nevertheless, their stories are extraordinary stories because life is extraordinary. Every life is the journey of a soul on this earth, a sacred soul, and every soul is extraordinary. Every human being is a mysterious creature, as mystical as our Lord Jesus is. I have heard, and I believe, that we are spirits passing through this earth with an important job to do. Unfortunately, only few of us will have the privilege to wait peacefully for the moment to see God face to face. Those people are the enlightened ones, like my friend and protector in heaven Padre Pio of Pietrelcina, Italy. He could hardly wait to die and go meet his beloved Jesus. In his life he was chosen to glorify Jesus and bore for fifty years the stigmata, the visible wounds of Christ. But most of us fear this moment because every human being fears death. Even Jesus told the Father, "If you can, pass this cup," but being also divine, He said, "Your will be done, not mine." With our relative minds, none of us are in a hurry to discover what is waiting for us. We fear the unknown, and this is precisely why I say, "Lord I believe, help my unbelief."

We humans are always wishing for something more. There is no limit to our wanting because our souls are copies of God's own spirit, and "only the absolute God can fulfill our hearts and soul." I'm repeating what St. Augustine already said, because his words became my motto. I truly believe them. My prayer today is, "Lord give me a content heart." A content heart has the Lord's peace in it. I am not speaking about God, as a doctor in theology would speak, I am speaking with the language of love, the language and the faith that I learned from my Grandmother when I was a little girl. I am speaking from simple faith, and I am telling you my story from the heart.

My young brother Alvinho had a remarkable life. It was full of victories, joy, love and accomplishments, but all of this came to a halt when he faced defeat by AIDS. Throughout his life he was a happy and positive person, sometimes he seemed to be carefree but he was always full of understanding and love for humanity. We all witnessed his concerns for social justice. He was a kind soul, a sensitive one. His body was destroyed by the tragedy of AIDS, however, he was a beautiful spirit. He made his mark on this earth among the people who were privileged to know him. He will not be forgotten as long as we, his loving family, lives. My nieces Moema and Valeria, my brother Joao Bosco, my sister Fatima and myself, will forever remember him.

Alvinho's concern and worries about the social and economic differences in Brazil were fundamental when it was time for him to choose a career. He used to say to me that we were responsible for the poor, but that we were the product of our society. We were part of a society that he did not understand because its structure was made of injustice and oppression. Not too many people were aware of this truth or cared to find out about it. He told me that we considered ourselves good and just. However, a large part of the people were selfish creatures, and even good people sometimes unconsciously were contributing to the social injustice as well. He also believed that people were divided into the givers and the takers, and we couldn't change this equation. He believed we all were guilty one way or the other because we were choosing to not see the reality of the poor. I knew that this rationale bothered him profoundly because he wanted to make a difference.

He wanted, as an attorney, to be able to help the less privileged. He also said that we had become blind to it all, our collective conscience had become numb, and somehow we needed to wake up soon, because we were all in the same boat. If not for the love of God, it must be done for the love of humanity. He was afraid that someday the abandoned children of the slums throughout Brazil would become the hard core criminals of our streets. We no longer would be able to live our lives in peaceful coexistence with the less privileged. It would be war between the ones who had and the ones who had not. Alvinho talked about social injustice with passion; he wanted a better world for everybody. He wanted to make an impact on the lives of the poor helping them live their lives with dignity.

He had a pure heart, perhaps he was too good to be living on this earth; I'm starting to believe that the good die young. Sad to say, my brother was right, and later on, twenty years later to be precise, the abandoned child of the favelas, (Brazilian's slums,) are now out on the streets living by the only creed, the only value that was taught to them, the only lesson learned on the streets, and unfortunately the lesson was survival through violence. they had to either cooperate with the drug dealers or face death. Alvinho used to say, "Whatever they do, they do for one reason only, it's for survival. Unfortunately today the streets of Brazil have become a dangerous jungle."

I ask myself, what do we do? We are all very good at still pretending to be blind to the problems, pretending that we are not responsible, placing blame on everybody and everything else but ourselves. We are the good Christians who go to church every Sunday, and pray with a sleeping conscience. We do nothing to change the status quo. It makes me think, what have I done Lord with the talent that You gave to me? What have I done to help the poor children who live in the streets of my country? Nothing. I did nothing.

I left Brazil and came to the United States of America looking for the promised land, trying to forget the horror of the abandoned children of Brazil, trying to forget the hurts of my own childhood. However, in my childhood, I wasn't always in misery. I had wonderful times playing in our backyard with my sisters and friends. I also had some memories of vacation in Baldum, the sugar mill that belonged to our cousin Bibi. These were times that even now I go back in time, and review in my mind and soul, that wonderful time. My sisters and I going down the river. The waters were up to our waists. When I was eight years old, the river wasn't very deep. From far away the waters of the river looked like green, there was sugar cane planted on both sides of the river. It was going like a snake, turning and turning and finally passing through the Mill. There we went to play and swim. It was heaven! Until today, remembering those times, I feel happy and blessed. Today, it soothes my soul.

I came to the United States of America, in pursuit of happiness. I had no idea that my life was going to be very difficult. I had no idea of my struggles. I had to assimilate a completely different culture. My Ingles were very limited. One time I wanted to buy something for dinner, at the store, I saw a can with a picture of chicken legs on it. I thought this would be perfect. I bought a can of chicken, when I opened it was a can of Crisco lard. I cried in misery. When Bill came home and saw my miserable state, he took us out to dinner. Bill was a handsome man of 39 years old. He was 12 years older than me. I was a naive girl, he was an experienced man. However, I had a destiny to fulfill. I believed that America was my destiny. I believed in America I could forget my pains. I was a young lady, full of dreams. I could finish my Law school, I thought, however reality was different. Here in the US, I found out I had to go back to undergrad school and after, applied for law. It was going to be a long time in school. I decided that I could go to a college and finish my education. At those times I had no idea of American reality, nor of my fiancé's financial situation. Even then, I took the chance, and left home. However I always pray, "Lord, guide me, show me the best road. Have mercy on me, a sinner! Help me to help others in need, help me never to say I can't when I see an open hand asking for help." I always ask for the Lord's help.

What I have learned from my first theologian, my grandma Titida, is to do charity on earth. It is the only road to salvation. Today I still think about the abandoned children of Brazil. This was always in my mind. Now I think about these children globally and I know that a child is a child, is a child. Wherever I am, I can always help. This rationale gave me peace of mind. There are so many children in this world without childhood; my heart still aches when I think about them. This was the reason why I decided to become a teacher. Alvinho always talked about abandoned children, and I believe that his heart also hurt for them because he understood them so well. My brother had a sensitive soul. He was also a naïve child of God.

****

Writing about Alvinho is telling about my deepest feelings and my family's profound pain and suffering. It is remembering when sadly we began witnessing day by day his ascent into Calvary, until his last breath. It's also my journey through life, my fears, hurts, joys and struggles.

My life Is the life of a Brazilian immigrant living in the United States of America. Now it's my spirit yelling in a last attempt to be understood by my daughters. I hope that someday by reading about my childhood, they will understand the reason for some of my mistakes and unfounded suspicions about child molestation. How traumatized I was about this subject at a very small age. In a way how my sisters and I were also victims, as we were exposed to kind of abuse, not being victimized ourselves but by knowing about it and how it happened in our own home.

Here I am also making my last plea for forgiveness to my husband. It is my last loud cry to let my daughters know that all I did was for love and to protect them. Unfortunately, in an attempt to protect my children, I made one of the biggest mistakes of my life and almost destroyed my own American family. I blamed my husband for something that never happened in our home. It only happened in my mind because of my traumatized childhood. And worst of all is that when I was trying to protect my daughters, I hurt them most. Perhaps I traumatized my own daughters. I live my life with this guilt. Unfortunately, I know better than anybody else how this kind of trauma stays with a person. Humbly I say to my husband and children, I am sorry. I am sorry. I am so very sorry. Please forgive me.

My accusations did hurt us all so much. It was a no win situation., we all lost. I almost broke our family, but destiny or karma kept us together. My husband's forgiveness gave us a second chance, and I took that chance with humility. I learned from my terrible mistake. I realized that life was the best university and that I had only one life to learn. I wouldn't have the chance to come back a second time and fix it.

And with every day I learned humility, I learned not only how to accept forgiveness, but also in the process, I learned to become more compassionate towards others. I became a more understanding and forgiving person myself. In other words, I began to understand the true meaning of Christian love. I began to heal my traumatized soul. At a very young age my nanny told me that my father was molesting her.

My nanny was 19 years old, when I was seven. Later I realized that she was abusing my sisters and me verbally, emotionally and physically because she was making us pay for our father's abusive actions towards her. She took revenge on us, three innocent girls.

Now, many years later I am making the connection with my past and my present life. I'm finding out how much damage memories of an unhappy childhood did to me. Not only affecting my past but also hurting my present life. Unfortunately it affected the people I love most in this life: my daughters, my husband. I'm sure of the negative impact it must have made in my sisters' lives also. We were all victimized. Later on I let my past experiences hurt my husband and daughters. My family, who I love so much.

Perhaps I'm being too bold and naive writing about my life, but in this process I am trying to understand my little brother's unnecessary death, his senseless death. My own mistakes, in a way to say again and again, Moema, Gina, I adore both of you, for the love of God, forgive me.

I'm trying to make sense of the suffering of my family and my own suffering, my trajectory through this earth. With my failures and successes, faults and virtues, I have come to a ripe age. I hope the good Lord will enlighten me, let me understand other people's errors. Bless our simple life helping my daughters and grandchildren. I don't know if I will be able to achieve my goal or if I will end my story without coming to understand about this journey that we call life. All I can do is try. How terrible, I hurt my mother when I came to the US. My sister said to me that my mom never stopped suffering, because I had left Brazil. She had missed me all her life. For all the sorrows I caused my Mom, I ask forgiveness, to my Lord and savior.

Perhaps it will be better to let my memories go with me to my final destination and yet I think. If it could help my daughters understand me a little better later on. If as a result it could shorten the gap between us, between my culture and theirs. If I could feel that they were proud of me, then it would be worth trying. Because of my daughters and my grandchildren, I accepted this challenge. I will gamble and take the risk. And if at the end I lacked the gift of communication, right now I ask them their forgiveness

Again, with humility I ask the Lord for his guidance. And remembering, I am trying to tell you about the 'best of times and the worst of times''. Again I will talk about Alvinho.

Alvinho was crazy about parties and I remember jokingly telling him that he was a party animal, because he loved to party so much and every day was a great day, life was a party. The Brazilian Carnaval was his favorite. Every year he went with friends to Salvador, capital State of Bahia, for a week of fun. At Carnaval everything and only the present would count. I also remember having lots of fun at Carnaval, but in my days it was different because it was a family party. I also remember at Carnaval, my friends and I went to the Bishop's house. We were using our masks trying to scare and surprise the good old Bishop. He would laugh, waiting patiently for us to remove our masks, then he would tell the maid to serve soda and cookies for us. Now everything has changed, and life has become a dangerous adventure. Nobody could do this anymore, not in Brazil, not anywhere. With the passage of years, Carnaval became a pagan dangerous party.

My brother never used drugs, but he liked to drink socially-good wine and good beer especially at Carnaval. Although, he was a responsible professional and never had a drinking problem. I suspect that it was at one of these crazy Carnival parties in Salvador, the capital of Bahia, that my brother was infected with the AIDS virus, but I will never know for sure.

******

"If you want to be famous sing about your village"

For some unknown reason, in 1960 in Brazil, some people in my hometown thought the world was going to end. Most of these people were uneducated and superstitious. Everyone else, including us college kids, were laughing about it. My friends and I were having fun sharing this idea with a few American Marines who were in my hometown. I was told that some of these boys were sons of influential politicians in America who were avoiding the war in Vietnam. I don't know if there is any truth in these stories. It was common knowledge in my town at that time. In this group of American young Marines there was one lieutenant, a captain and a sergeant in charge, but it was the sergeant, who the American boys feared most. When the sergeant came to the beach to drink with the boys, we could feel the tension among them. My friends and I were at the beach joining the Americans, Life was a big party.

When I met Bill in 1966, I didn't realize that my life was going to change dramatically, and that he was the man of my life. Because of him I decided to come to the USA, I didn't totally realize what I was doing. Leaving my whole life behind when I left Brazil. My beloved city, Natal, who was a tropical paradise. Its beaches with white sand, coconut trees, exotics palm trees and delightful weather, it was the jewel of the Northeast. I can only see Natal, my hometown, with the eyes of the beloved.

Natal is an old city with the Atlantic Ocean bathing its coasts. This city was born involved in a legend, the legend of the Three Wise Man. The legend says that when a Portuguese man, named Jeronimo de Albuquerque, discovered Natal around Christmas time and the baby Jesus was the one who pointed to him the safe port of Natal. For this reason Albuquerque named this town Natal, which means Christmas in Portuguese language. Natal was born on this same day under the shadow of the holy crib, in honor of our Lord Jesus Christ. In Natal the ocean is untamed like a wild horse and is intensely green as an emerald. The ocean in Natal shines like the most beautiful and precious emerald. The beaches are beautifully white, the days are warm, and the nights are cool. It feels like it is summer all year around. We call Natal the city of the sun because it doesn't rain there very much. In Natal the summer mornings at the beach under the wonderful sun, were unforgettable.

I can't write poetically enough about the sun, I can only tell how I felt it, because I felt so much alive under the sun. I felt happy beyond imagination when I ran down from the top of the dunes. Feeling the warm sand in my feet and legs I was free as the birds in the sky. Looking at the sun shining over the land, the green Atlantic ocean water, and the blue sky above, I was truly alive. The sunshine made the beach a true wonderland, everything was healthy, vibrant and lively. In Natal the waters of this immense emerald ocean are warm throughout the whole year and one can swim day or night. If one chooses to swim at night, sometimes the moon comes out covering everything with its white rays, letting one feel at peace; giving the impression of an eternal Christmas night, bringing into us peace of mind and soul.

Natal is a place where one can feel at peace because it seems that all of the wonders of nature are there. One can feel the grandeur of our Creator at day or at night. There the soul strongly feels in communion with God through nature. Natal is for us a real Christmas gift, beautiful all year around. This city of wonders can also offer a complete surprise in the inner city. When a bold visitor risks going into the inner city where the underprivileged poor people live, he finds there too much poverty and suffering. Among the poor, life is difficult. They work hard, some of them trying to sell their products at the beaches where the tourists, the rich and privileged are playing and enjoying the ocean, taking life easy. Sometimes the vendors become a pest, trying to sell their goods. Other times they become comedians and entertain the tourists by dancing and singing. At the same time they offer their CDs, most of the time not of good quality. These CDs are overpriced and purchased at the black market. However, one must know the city to be able to love it and to understand and feel its magic.

Natal, with its breathtaking view of the Via Costeira, is a colorful city, with its green ocean and immense white dunes, deep green tropical vegetation and blue skies with its radiant white clouds. Natal is unique. It is a dream and reality, it's life abundance. Natal is light and shadows, and in Natal one can feel life at its fullest. On the streets, among many tropical fruits and exotic flowers, we still find ancients baobabs with their gigantic trunks and enormous foliage. One of them is kept as a sacred relic because the people believe in the legend that it was under this baobab tree that the French writer, Antoine de Saint Exupery was inspired and wrote his famous book The Little Prince. Some historians say that in 1942 during the Second W World

War, this author worked for the post office, flying his airplane from Dakar, Senegal to Natal, because it was the shortest point from Africa when flying across the Atlantic. At this time Senegal was a French colony.

What is true is that under the baobabs and the mango trees in our neighborhood, many girls exchanged kisses and promises of eternal love. Many young girls after a love night under those trees ended up nine months later, holding a blond baby in their arms, a product of the war. My father said, "a war casualty.'

For these American babies made in Brazil, and their mothers, there was only one road to take, it was a career at Maria Boa's house, the local whorehouse. There was no opportunity in town for a young girl from a good family, who was impregnated by an American G. I. or, in fact, by anybody else. As a matter of fact, virginity was a precious thing to save for marriage. Many girls were returned to their homes the day after their wedding because their husbands found out that they weren't virgins.

I knew the story of my father's cousin, my second cousin, who had lost her virginity when she was engaged. When the engagement broke up she was without her most precious gift, her virginity. She didn't despair and she became engaged to someone else. She married this other man, and on her wedding night, before she got in bed with her groom, she had a bottle of red dye, they said it was Mercurochrome, hidden under the pillowcase. When the time came for him to have some intimacy, she cried out that she was very shy and asked him to turn off the light, and so he did. She started making loud noises so that all the maids heard the commotion. When her husband turned the light on again, there were the sheets with lots of red blood for him to see. Quickly she pulled off the sheets. The next day, cousin Maria instructed the maid to throw away the sheets because the dye would not come out. Her marriage was a successful one. She had three daughters, was happily married for many years and made her husband a happy man. But everybody in the family knew her story, and this old story was told over and over again, of how smart cousin Maria was to be able to pull a trick like that, saving her honor and her family honor too. All the girls in our family believed this old story. However, when cousin Maria heard about it for the first time, she swore that it was a vicious lie, and she maintained it was a lie until the day she died. Unfortunately for her, nobody believed her version of the story.

****

My hometown had extraordinary beauty but the people lacked beauty in open-mindedness. For this reason my grandmother used to say, "God doesn't give everything to the same people. He gave us this beautiful place but look at the narrowness of some people's mind towards women's freedom and rights. I know for sure that ten of these men aren't worth one good woman." I truly love my grandma.

Our society demanded women to save our virginity for our husbands. However, if a poor woman became a virgin spinster, this same society would laugh at her, making fun of the old lady. However, if a woman became a whore, she was a worthless bitch. It was a no-win situation for women. A married or single man had the right to visit a whorehouse any time he wanted, but if a wife or girlfriend had an affair, he also had the right to defend his honor, most of the time by putting a bullet into his wife's or girlfriend's head. It was accepted because he was defending his honor. In my hometown, in the sixties, justice was really blind; the scale always tilted towards the man. One could ask how about women's honor and rights? How about them? I have heard that today this situation has changed for the better. Just after the divorce was implemented. However, I have my doubts about how much the rights of a woman are respected in my hometown, because many men of my generation are still following the book of their fathers. It is the same among politicians; they follow the old corrupt ways.

****

I heard many of these stories about Natal from my Grandma. She told me some of these stories in our backyard under the avocado or guava tree. Other stories were told at bedtime. Some of Vovo's stories about Natal were not too edifying. She told me about booming whorehouses and famous madams, especially Maria Boa's whorehouse, the most famous or infamous of these times. The owner's name was Maria, "A casa de Maria Boa", (Good Maria's house). It became famous and prosperous because of the American soldiers in Natal during wartime, but also because all the important men in town were customers of Maria Boa. They used Maria Boa's whorehouse for pleasure, drinking and conducting business.

One day my father told my mom that he had to go to Maria Boa's house for business. He sent people from his office to investigate the liquor business, and he had to supervise because Maria Boa was refusing to cooperate with the tax men sent there by my father. However it ended up in a big fight between Mom and Father, when Vovo Titida told my mother that she didn't believe at all that it was all about business, because Father had brought mom a box of her favorite powder as a present. She told mom that Maria Boa had given my father a present too. And the next thing I saw was the box of powder flying in the backyard, white powder all over the place. My father was "in the dog house" for a few days. There was never lost love between them. They just tolerate each other.

Vovo Titida told me about the people who made their living selling the trash left behind by the American soldiers. For this reason everybody in town believed that there was no poverty in America. My father used to say, "we can find out quite a lot about a nation,

through its trash. These foreigners do waste a great deal. America must be a wealthy nation."

My father considered the young Brazilian girls, who were emotionally involved with the American soldiers "war casualties" because their lives were totally wasted after their love affairs with the young GIs ended. Grandma said that one could see in a dark night, some girls' shadows, with their bodies so close to their boyfriends that they looked like one. They hugged and kissed under the baobabs trees throughout the city, or inside the cemeteries with no fear or respect for the dead. These young girls, I was told, had to go in a hurry to a gynecologist, only to find out they were pregnant. This explained to me why some of my girlfriends were blond, in a land of brown faces. This always puzzled me as a kid, but I never asked any questions.

Some Brazilian young men also dated American nurses. I remember a story that I heard one night, from a Law School professor, a prominent man. He told me his love story with an American nurse. He was very relaxed drinking beer at his beach house, and I was there with a group of my friends from the University. At the time he was, in my opinion, an old man, but he was probably in his fifties, about my father's age. He had offered his beach house, at Ridinha Beach, for our class to have a weekend party, and he later decided to enjoy our company. None of us, his students, were too crazy about the idea, but what could we do? We needed his beach house, so we accepted the house for our party and with the house came the professor. That night at the party, he told me that a baby boy was the result of his love affair with an American nurse and that she had to go back to the United States to give birth to his child. Years later the boy came to Natal looking for his father, but things didn't work out, because his Brazilian wife was very jealous about the whole story. I guess he forsook his son, because at the time he had two other sons with his Brazilian wife. I thought it was a sad story of human weakness. I couldn't help feeling sorry for this American/Brazilian boy, and I thought, like my father used to think, he, too, was a war casualty because he was so badly rejected by his own father. Immediately after listening to my professor's story I couldn't help feeling disgusted with his action and somehow I couldn't respect him anymore. But I kept his story to myself, sharing it only with my Vovo Titida, because he was well known and respected in our town. I believe, when he told me his story, he was totally drunk.

That night I saw this old man crying like a baby, perhaps with true regrets or in the effect of lots of beer. Why this professor told me his love story I really don't know, all I knew was that he was respected at the academic level and well known in our society. But that night he seemed to become very vulnerable. He cried for his son and for his lost love, or perhaps all the beer that he drank made him melancholy. I always wondered. I didn't enjoy being his confidant; he made me feel very uncomfortable. However, any story about Americans in Natal always fascinated me, and I listened with interest.

That night this professor also became a little comic, or perhaps pathetic would be a better word. He had a beer belly, and was trying his best to keep it flat. We could see that once in a while he tried to hide it pulling his belly in, but we all noticed he wasn't being successful in his efforts. Because of his silly behavior my friends and I had a good laugh at his expense, but right there I promised myself, if I lived long enough to be old, in his case middle age, I would act my age, I wouldn't be ridiculous. After this beach party we started calling him, behind his back of course, "peacock". I hope no one else ever finds out who this fellow professor was, because he is probably long gone from this earth but his family is a well-known and prestigious family who still lives in my hometown.

There were some people with other peculiar behavior at this party. One of my girlfriends drank a little too much, and when we looked for her she was swimming in the ocean with her boyfriend, and they were naked as jaybirds. Unfortunately for me, someone told my mother about this party, and my mother came to talk to me visibly upset and crying, thinking that I, too, was doing things that she couldn't approve of. I tried to put my mom at ease, and explained to her that I was still a good girl, that I was there without a boyfriend, and that my girlfriend Dalvanira and I were dumping all the liquor that we could into the sand. I told my mother the truth; we tried to stop the heavy drinking that was going on to avoid a disaster from happening. We had to drive back home with some of our friends, who were already drunk. I believe we had strong guardian angels because we didn't have a car accident that night. At home I thanked God for bringing me home safely. Thanks to my mother, my father never found out about this party, thanks be to God, because I would be dead meat if he had known.

****

As a young girl I was fascinated with the stories about Americans in my hometown. I asked my mom why she hadn't married an American soldier like so many other girls had done. She told me it was because she was already in love with my father. And she couldn't understand their language. It sounded worse than Louro's talk (Louro was our parrot.) I thought to myself, too bad. Everyone in The American movie industry did a good job too. The American soldiers were heroes in Natal. However, when I arrived in the USA, things were different. In Natal people were saying, '' In America, the wives come first, then the kids, the dogs and the husband come last. "It wasn't the reality here. The difference was, women had their rights. I found out that husbands were unfaithful too. However when wives did the same, they were not killed. I told my husband. '' Bill, we have the same rights, if you find another woman, stay with her, don't come back to me, I will understand, because if you come back, I will do the same to you. What is good for the goose, is good for the gander. I would never do the same, because of my beliefs and my faith, for me it did not make sense.

The only reason I would sleep with a man, was if I loved and lived with him. I wouldn't ever take that kind of revenge, for me it didn't make any sense. However, my husband never knew that. I want him to be careful, and think that I would do it. Today I tell the same for my daughters. "If your husband does something wrong, ignore it if you can, or leave him, and take your kids with you" After that you can find another partner. However, never dishonor your name and your children."

BACK TO MY CHILDHOOD. When we were seven or eight years old, every Saturday my sisters and I went to the movie theater to watch Tarzan's serial. Later on as teenagers we loved to cry watching the movie "Love is a many splendored thing", sighing over William Holden's performance and dreaming with James Dean and Elvis Presley, they were my idols.

At that time, the people in my hometown said that America was the place to live because everybody in America had a car and were rich, or middle class. In Texas everybody owned oil wells, people were millionaires, and everything was big. You could find oil in your own backyard. That was the way that everybody went from rags to riches. The poor people in America had a jeep, a house and a radio. No one had to take a bus. My father enlightened us about the truth. He told us that almost all these stories were products of imagination. There was no paradise on earth and everything was relative. We shouldn't believe the tales. But many people believed those stories and dreamed about living in America to escape poverty. My father said that America was powerful and a good country in which to live, because the laws were respected and the people had a voice. I listened attentively to his words. Now I understand, the laws here are better than ours in Brazil. However in any place in this world, the power is in the hands of the wealthy.

When I became an adolescent, the material riches of America did not impress me too much. What impressed me the most about

America was to hear about people's freedom, and the respect for human rights. Public opinion was a serious issue because in Brazil at that time the public had no opinion. My father said that the judicial system was one of the best in the world, and for some reason I believed it to be true. I had to carefully separate the tall tales that were told in my town from the truth, but I deeply believed in freedom and justice in America because of my grandma's stories about World War II and my father's conversation about America.

It was in my hometown Natal that the Americans had fought for freedom in the world and had won it for everyone. Grandma Titida told me Americans were flying from Natal to Africa, and since then American soldiers have become my heroes. The battles for freedom fought by American soldiers, from Natal in 1942, on the African campaign, were never forgotten in my home. There were incredible stories circulating about the Brazilian girls who married American soldiers. Some said that they were invited to the White House to have dinner with the president or became friends with the famous. The simple people in town believed it as if it were holy gospel. My father laughed at these tales, saying that the American people probably would believe that we, the people from Natal, were still practicing cannibalism, and the Brazilian girls were wearing fireflies on their hair at night, to help them to see in the dark. Some people in America probably believed these silly stories too.

However, I paid attention when my father and his friends talked about social justice in Brazil and in America. They compared it, saying that in America the poor had assistance, and that few suffered from hunger. They said that health care and the political democratic system were also the best in the world. My father always spoke about the freedom in America wishing to see the same freedom in Brazil. He said that the people had true freedom of speech, and only in America could one celebrate such freedom because the people had conquered it and defended it with their own blood. There "the pen was mighty thankful to the sword, and the sword to the pen," because everything had started with an idea from the brain into the paper and from the paper into action. At that time my dad used to make the words of the poet Augusto dos Anjos, his words, asking "Ideas, where do they come from? From what raw material?"

I would ask myself, ideas, where do they come from? I knew they came from parts of our brain, but how? How were they created? Sometimes things got too complicated for my young mind, but the important lesson to me was that freedom, we don't beg and we don't trade. Freedom we conquer. Americans had conquered their freedom with bravery and honor, with the blood of their young people. I was told by my old friend Seu Luis Flor, who at the time of the war, as a young men, was working with the Americans in Parnamirim Field, driving his truck, he said that some Americans came inside bags from Africa to Natal and from Natal to the United States to be buried at home. These young American soldiers had made the ultimate sacrifice, had given their lives fighting for freedom in the world. I understood well how priceless freedom was.

Almost every night after dinner on our porch or inside our small library, my father and his friends would talk about many subjects. One of his favorites was French literature, and they always finish their conversation discussing French literature. In those nights I was always close enough to them listening to every single word, I was there nearby until somebody finding me there would reprimand me for listening to men's conversation. I listened to every word. Many times I took books from my father's library, books that had been discussed the night before. I read them even when I couldn't understand their content. Without understanding much, and without my father's knowledge I read every book in our library because I had developed a hunger for learning.

My father also said that an American could make any criticism about their president and continue to walk free. It was not so in our so-called democratic regime. Everybody was afraid to talk or write against the government. This American freedom, my father believed, was the result of true democracy and education. He said this because education was his Holy Grail, and he was saying that American political and judicial systems were so different then our political and judicial system, where crime and punishment was only for the poor and destitute. People with money made their own laws in Brazil. Today I found out that money and power can corrupt any political system.

These talks profoundly influenced me. When I was in college in the sixties, certain books were prohibited at the university libraries in Brazil. They were considered subversives, and the media could show or express only half-truths, nothing negative about the government was allowed. Every protest against the government had to be camouflaged, and songs were prohibited as being subversive too. At that time, I dreamed about the concept of justice and pursuit of happiness for all. The military dictatorship was happening in Brazil at the same time I was in college. I was a true and naïve idealist girl. After school I became a capitalist.

Years later when I came to live in America I grew up fast and found out that, here in America as in every place on earth, there was social injustice. Nevertheless even with its flaws, I still believe in the American judicial system. I also remember grandma Titida saying that real justice one could find only with the Lord our God because here down on this earth everything was relative, even justice. One more time Vovo Titida proved to be right.

Thanks be to God, every Sunday one can see churches of all faiths full of people, despite the malls and the internet. I do believe in the goodness and fairness of the American people, in their generosity towards all people because I have witnessed it. Every time there is a crisis in the world I see how charitable American people are. I admire the law of the land, the respect for its constitutional rights, and I still believe in the good USA. Today we are having hard economic times because in God we trust. We are proud and resilient people, we will be fine, and this too will pass.

However, when I was growing up in Brazil, the Brazilian government was the first one to show the Brazilian people how to lie, steal, be corrupt, and in this way achieve success. Any decent, honest government official was considered a moron or a fool and was laughed at. My own father was considered a fool because he did not take bribes when he was in charge of the IRS in my State, his title was "superintendent fiscal do Estado do Rio Grande do Norte". His friends called him "Cordeirinho," which means "Little lamb". This was part of his native American name. My grandfather's name. My father was a true diplomat outside our home. He was well respected and liked at work.

At this time, stealing from the Brazilian nation became a privilege of few and an art of the elected by the people. Fortunately for the country, the Brazilian people, despite the government, were working hard for their progress and for the progress of their country. It was the politicians who were learning year after year from the same old book of corruption. I remember Grandma repeating the stories about American soldiers who had fought for freedom. Some people, like Rosa Parks and President L. Johnson, had successfully worked toward this feat. She did it for her race; he did it for his political ambition, nevertheless freedom and opportunity for all people was expected. For me, America became the land where anyone could be successful; the land of opportunities. I was going to be successful. I wanted to be part of the last frontier, the frontier of the mind. I would be there someday, and I would study in an American university and I would get my degree. I never thought it was a crazy dream. I always saw myself holding my American diploma, my degree. Only today I have a name for this. I was visualizing my future, and I didn't know it at that time. Many times, my grandma had said to me, "wanting is power" but I wasn't aware of my inner power yet nor had I knowledge of the word visualization.

Now I turn my face toward my awesome God whom I also call Jesus, Holy Spirit, Love, Breath, Energy and Life and I ask, "Please Lord show me how to love." My sister, who says she is an atheist, insists that there is no God, that science can't prove the existence of a god. I asked her to show me how science can prove the non-existence of God, but she couldn't give me any good answer. Science can't prove that God does not exist; besides one either has the grace to believe or one doesn't. It's up to the Lord to give it to us, the gift of faith. We are empty vases, everything is a gift from above and for this reason, I am beginning to learn not to pass judgment. After all, what do I know? What do we know about somebody else's soul? Many times, we don't even understand ourselves. The best we can do is to act in our faith because faith is also action. Nirvana, Heavens or any other imaginary paradise, isn't achievable without love and charity because God is love and compassion and regardless of religion; without love and compassion God wouldn't exist. I learned this truth with Vovo Titida.

Jesus said, "My yoke is light." He made it possible for us to be happy regardless of our crosses or burdens but we need to believe in Him who is "the way, the truth and the life ''I learned that in America anyone who had talent was recognized, it was the opposite in my hometown, in the sixties, where, after finishing college, only the sons and daughters of the rich and privileged had a chance to occupy good jobs in the government.

When grandma Titida told me stories about the American soldiers in Natal, she said that in the 1940s, all the propaganda in

Brazil was good toward the USA. When American soldiers were in Natal fighting in the African campaign against German dictator A. Hitler, the people of Brasil were learning through newspapers, radio, magazines and documentaries about the consequences of the agreement between the American president, Mr. Roosevelt, and the Brazilian president, the dictator Getulio Vargas. The Brazilian president let the Americans have a military base in Natal in exchange for technological and financial help. In April 1941, the first project started, and in January 1942 the construction of the American base began. Grandma said it was the biggest American base outside US territory. Natal in 1943 had 40,000,00 inhabitants, plus 150,000 American soldiers, who were living at the American base. The base was named Parnamirim Field, and we Brazilians called it O Campo -The Field. The planes were bomber and cargo types. Many B-25s flew over town. The hydroplanes landed on the Potengy River, next to our home, much to the delight of the neighborhood kids. At night the population was asked to keep the lights dimmed at home, and the people obeyed because they feared an attack by the Germans. Natal was the closest point in South America to Senegal, Africa and its city Dakar, where the Americans had a military campaign waged against Hitler. For this reason, Natal was strategically vital for the Americans during World War II. I was told that in 1943 some bodies of the American boys were brought from Africa to Parnamirim to be sent home for burial, and that it was a sad thing to see the bodies of the young American soldiers inside bags ready to be shipped home. My Vovo Titida told me that in war there were no winners and that she felt sorry for the parents of these young boys. It was a great sacrifice and a high price to pay for freedom. The American planes were also repaired at the base with the help of some Brazilian mechanics. Many local young men found jobs in Parnamirim Field. My uncle Joao worked there as a mechanic. The base was well built, and even now it is in good working condition. The airport today is also in Parnamirim.

My mother remembered when the president of the United States, Mr. Roosevelt, came to Natal with his wife, Eleanor Roosevelt. She told me it was the event of the year. Many people came from Rio de Janeiro to Natal, to honor the couple as if they were royalty. For Brazil's technology and progress the support from the American government was also of vital importance. The Parnamirim base proved to be an excellent trade, for Brazil and for our allies, who were fighting for freedom and justice in the world. For us, the Brazilian people, Americans were our heroes, the good guys who were fighting for freedom in the world. They were our powerful friends, and the Brazilians students at the universities weren't considering the Americans in a negative way, as the police of the world, nor were they calling the Americans imperialists. It was in the sixties with the Vietnam War, that university students in Brazil became critical of American foreign policies and I was one among them.

The people in Natal were simple and hospitable people, and they didn't care about the Vietnam War. It was at the University that I was aware of the anti-American movement because of the trade industry and the Vietnam War. It was at the university that I first heard someone calling Americans imperialists. At that time the communist regime in Russia was considered a threat to Brazil and almost in every government office, especially at the post office, where you could see the anti-communist propaganda on the walls. The Brazilian people understood that communism was not good for Brazil, but the dictatorship wasn't either. In Brazil, it was the time for the people who had and those who had not, unfortunately the status quo never changed much, Brazil is still a country of those who have and have not. Unfortunately, communism is a utopia, for some people a beautiful utopia. But it is just that, the ideology, and the impossibility to come into practice. Jesus Christ himself, as a revolutionary, couldn't bring equality for all. He brought love, redemption, justice, but not economic social change for all. In his infinite wisdom he said, "give to Caesar what belongs to Caesar and to God what belongs to God. '' I came to believe that we need the poor as much as they need us because it is in helping others that we feel fulfillment and joy. As St. Therese once said, today we are God's heart, hands and feet here on earth. We are mystical people; how can we ever comprehend God's plan for us? My brother Alvinho had the gift of discernment; he could see the needs of others; he would perceive the needs of others before anybody could see them. I envy this gift because I, too, want to help, but I don't see the needs of others at first. One has to ask me for help before I see their needs, and I admire those who help before being asked to help. Alvinho never denied anyone the charity of a smile, a hug, a kiss, or his money. I believe for this reason he was so loved, and thought that his friends were all true friends, because he was a true friend for all of them, my little brother had a pure soul.

My brother Alvinho was born in Natal on August 6, 1960, when I was an adolescent. He was my bundle of joy, and my sisters and I loved him like he was our own child. He grew up happy and healthy and loved by every member of our family. When he was seven years old, I met my future husband, Bill, an American soldier who was tracking satellites at Barreira do Inferno, a military site near Natal. At this time, I was studying law, 1966, It was a hot summer night. I was coming from the University library, with two girlfriends, around 9pm, when I suggested, let's all go have some ice cream. "We went downtown to a favorite place called, '' Q-Show". When we got there, it was crowded. I saw Bill sitting having a drink. Two other men were there with him. I went up and down, looking at him, I said, in English, ''Let's go, there is no place to sit'' My friends, who did not speak English, said, ''are you crazy? "What are you saying? I said, this cute guy isn't Brazilian. They asked who? I said, "The one with green eyes. He looked at me and said, "Please, sit with us. Well, this was the beginning of my romance. Finishing my ice cream, I got up to go and he said, let me take you home. I said ''. Only if you take my friends and leave your friends here. '' In my head, I had done the equation, three young men, three girls in a foreign car. No way! He left his friends and took us home; however, I asked him to stop before my home. My parents would kill me, if they ever found out that I was coming home in an American car. Bill asked me if he could see me the next day and I said, yes. My father wasn't home, he was traveling, and my mom was easy to deal with. Then, I told my friends, "We will never see this fellow again, He probably is on a ship, tomorrow he will be gone. Tomorrow came, and at seven pm, he was at my door. I couldn't believe my eyes. When he met my mom, grandma and sisters, they were white and one of my sisters was blond. He asked me. "Are you adapted? I said no, I'm brown because my father is my color. We all laughed at him, when he left my home. I was really brown, because I went to the beach every day. Bill was very handsome; however, he was a foreign, twelve years older than me and divorced. Ttree strikes against him. I never told my family that he was divorced. They wouldn't allow me to date him. Fortunately, my sister and I were the only ones speaking English in our home at the time. I never told her he was divorced. When my father finally met Bill, my dad showed him his gun. After this first encounter, I told my mom, this guy will never come back here. Why did dad do that? Soon I found out why. My father started writing in magazines, books, in any paper available, that he was xenophobic, when I asked him what xenophobic was. He told me to look in the dictionary, the father of the donkeys. "burros "He was angry, says to me that I was in law school. It was a shame I didn't know.

Before I met Bill, in 1960 I dated an American GI, a marine, named Ken who was from Pennsylvania. One night at the beach he told me that he was going back to the United States. Perhaps because I was an emotional girl, I cried. That was enough for him to assume I was in love with him. He showed up a few months later at my doorstep, surprising me. He told me, "I have relisted because of you. Do you want to marry me?" Oh my God! I was in shock; I was already dating a Brazilian lieutenant in the air force.

Well, I wasn't thinking about marrying anybody yet. Marriage was not in my immediate plans. I was in college, and I wanted my career first. I told Ken no, I wasn't ready for marriage, and he flew into a rage saying, "I reenlisted. I have relisted because of you!"

Dear Lord, today I realize what he did and now I totally understand his sacrifice and what I did to that poor boy. I hope he survived Vietnam and that he is now a happy grandpa in Pennsylvania.

About Alvinho

On dark nights the sky would offer everybody a tapestry of bright stars, with the Southern Cross shining beautifully among other constellations. I always loved to look at it; for me it was a sign of peace, a sign of God's covenant with us. It was an assurance that God would always be with us and that Jesus was Lord. I often thought looking at the Southern Cross that Rio de Janeiro had its statue of Christ the redeemer, a gift from France, but Natal had the Southern Cross, a gift from God. It was more beautiful and more meaningful than anything else. I looked at it as a sign of true blessing, and on nights of full moon, nature offered us another beautiful and different spectacle. The moon rose from the ocean looking like a shining gold medal. It bathed the land, covering everything with its white light. On these nights I liked to stay under the moonlight, letting its rays come over me, caressing my skin. Some nights, when the moon was bathing in the waters of the Potengy River, a river close to my home, it was like a mystical experience for me. On these moonlit nights I lived moments of awakening and enlightenment. I didn't know how to pray at these times, I didn't understand my feelings. I felt good, I felt peaceful, but I also felt something more, something that I couldn't totally comprehend or describe even today. Now I know and understand that what I wanted to say to my God was, for Him to help me to die to myself and let Him live in me, I felt the magic of the moment, but I didn't yet have the maturity to understand what my immortal soul wanted. I just stood there in awe looking up at the universe and feeling part of a miracle, the incomprehensive miracle of life. The moon also always reminded me of one of mother's favorite songs,

"My silver hair are serenade kisses that the moon sent to me, and the kisses were so pure, that my dark hair became white like the moon"

My mother was also moonstruck like I was and as romantically inclined as I, but it was only under the influence of the moonlight that she revealed a little of her romantic side. Singing her favorite song delighted all of us. My sweet and humble mother, who I unintentionally made suffer so much because of my choices in life. I want now to ask her for forgiveness. Grandma used to say that God makes you die to yourself and makes you live in Him, that this is the principle of our faith, our Christianity, because we were made from God and some day we all will return to Him. Later on, my priest wrote. "God is the goal of all destinations."

I believe that my mother learned how to die to herself when she accepted all her sufferings; she transformed herself into Christ. I do believe that all who accept their sufferings learn how to die to themselves and learn how to live in Him, this eternal mystery that we call God, Christ, positive energy or love itself. However, I never understood this truth when I was at home in Brazil. I was an immature young lady, and it was only when I was away from home that I grew up fast.

Many nights at the beach house, I watched the game played by the clouds with the moon. A cloud would cover the moon for one moment, and by the next it would pass letting the moon reappear again like the queen of the night, in total control of her kingdom. I stayed for hours looking at the movement of the clouds. They were moving fast, with their sister coming behind covering and uncovering the moon over and over. Changing their shapes and again passing by one by one, pushed away by the wind. I quietly waited for the moon to reappear in all its splendor; its rays covering the ocean and the sand, taking over the town, bathing our body and souls with its cool light.

As a child I looked at the moon and saw Saint Jorge and the dragon. The dragon was always under St. Jorge's spear. I loved to look at St. Jorge's moon with Grandma, my sisters and our friends. We talked a lot about the dragon. Each of us is full of confidence in St. Jorge's protection. These nights in Natal were grand and mysterious for my sisters and me.

My mother and a few other ladies always gave food after supper to some people who lived down the street. We thought it was normal to do. I grew up seeing my mother and other neighbors taking care of the less privileged. At that time, I learned that sharing was a normal thing to do.

On our street there was an old colored man named Antonio. He showed up one day carrying a bag on his back and asking for food. He was unusually tall and bow legged. My mother gave him some food, and the next day the neighbor gave him more food, and soon he started sleeping on everybody's porch. It didn't take long for the people to get used to his presence. Some people started calling him Mr. Antonio of the streets, and the people made him our street security. However, he was an old man who never carried a gun, but for us he was an old, gentle giant. Mr. Antonio was homeless. We all knew this, but we never found out much about his life before he came to our street. For some strange reason this didn't matter, and he was immediately accepted in our neighborhood. He became our bowlegged black angel, and we believed that he was protecting our homes and us. He did not have a humble spirit; he never acted like a grateful beggar. He was a proud man who would discuss any subject with my father and was sure of his convictions. He was smart, could read and write, but we didn't know much about his formal education. He was a very private man; nobody ever knew about his life.

Mr. Antonio loved to complain about the food that the people gave him for dinner. This would make all the ladies of our street angry, and my mother was no exception. One day he sat inside our porch next to my father, with a heavy face, and my father asked, "Are you hungry Mr. Antonio?"

He said, "I just don't feel well, Mrs. Raimundinha, your neighbor, gave me a piece of bread. It was so old that they must have served it at the Last Supper."

Then my father got up and went to the kitchen looking for my mother and said, "Please make a plate with food for Mr. Antonio. He's on our porch and he has a hungry face."

My mother said no, she wasn't going to feed him anymore, because he was an ungrateful soul. She said that he always complained about her food to the neighbors, and that he didn't appreciate the good food that people were giving him.

My father replied, "But he is hungry."

That was all that was necessary to be said. My mother gave him dinner again and again, and the neighbors did just the same. Mr. Antonio's complaints became a joke among our neighbors, we all knew that he would complain about the food that was given to him, but for some reason, nobody got offended anymore. We all learned to love him the way he was, with his arrogance and peculiar ways, he was accepted among us. He loved to play the numbers and lost all his little money playing. Sometimes when he did win, he would buy a new hat, shoes, clothes and an umbrella, only to a few days later sell everything to play the numbers again and again lose it all.

He lived on our street for many years. I was a child when he came to live on our street, and when I left to come to the United States, he was still there. I remember running down the streets of my childhood, barefooted and carefree, and Mr. Antonio reminded.

me to be careful, but the harder he tried to make me stop, the faster I ran, laughed, and tried to be faster than the wind. When I came to the United States, I left him behind, and with him some happy memories of my childhood. When he died, I was living in Tucson, Arizona. I learned that our next-door neighbor Mr. Luis and my brother Bosco helped bury him. He was our friend, and I was happy that my brother had helped, giving him a Christian burial, otherwise his destitute body would be donated to the University Hospital, where the young medical students were studying anatomy. Nobody in our street wanted that to happen to him because on our street everybody was considered family.

Our neighborhood was made of some middle class and some very poor people, in fact half of the houses in the upper part of the street were the homes of merchants, politicians and government officials, like my father, the other half were the homes of seamstresses, street vendors and maids. One could see clearly the difference in these social classes, but playing on the street, we never saw any difference at all. Everybody there was friends and everyone knew about everybody else's business. We were like a happy family. The right for privacy was something that I learned years later here in the United States. I guess I became Americanized and now I like my privacy. Looking back, I miss some of the good days of my childhood, I try to keep them in a special place in my memory and at the same time I keep suppressing the bad ones.

From my mom I learned to go to nature to find God. Like she used to say, recharge my battery. When I asked my mom why she was alone under the trees, she answered, "Because here I can converse with God. Under these trees, I find peace, and I recharge my batteries''." At that time, I didn't pay much attention to what she was saying, but years later, married and in a foreign country with two young daughters, I also found the need to recharge my batteries. Like my mother I went to my backyard under the orange tree to seek the peace and strength to carry on with my duties as wife and mother.

At these times my vertical conversation with God was from my heart to His, and it was always about my family and me. Years later I learned how to pray for the needs of the community and for the needs of all. I realized we were all one big family; the family of God and receiving Him in the sacrament of holy communion helped me with my new vision of Christianity. I finally understood that the son of God, my Cosmic Jesus, shed his blood for all mankind, for Christians, Muslim and Jews. In that moment on, my conversation with God became action for myself, for my family and for others. I began living in harmony with the universe because God is universal and Omnipotent, He is in all places.

I have lived long enough to come to the conclusion that the worst sin is a social sin. It is injustice done to others. It is the indifference and absence of involvement with certain social issues. I became more aware and fearful of what someone else was calling social justice. Some people were justifying the exploitation of other human beings and children were still doing hard labor overseas, and we unconsciously bought the product of their labor because the goods made overseas would cost less.

Issues like abortion and illegal immigrants who were dying trying to cross the American desert of Arizona began to really bother me, forcing me to think. These immigrants without papers were not criminals or drug dealers but just ordinary people, hardworking people, only trying to have a better life in America. These issues became bothersome to me because I am sure that God hears the cry of the poor. This great nation of immigrants can't ignore this problem, because ignoring the poor is against America's principles, it's totally un-American. I see the American government as part of the solution for this problem. The Government needs to find a humanitarian solution to this problem. Why not create a working program for the people who need jobs here? This was done before, at the time of World War II and it worked. Why not try it again? We should learn from history, let's read history books again if necessary. The border issue isn't only a government issue; it's everybody's issue, everyone who has a Christian conscience. But here I am again, thinking and doing nothing about it. The only way I can change something is by voting for the candidate who has a compassionate heart towards these issues and by praying, because we never know when they are elected and in power, if their views will change.

Today I seek the love of God more than ever, hoping that He will be one with me. Hoping that He is helping me to create something positive in my life. At the same time learning how to share with the less privileged, who are my brothers and sisters in Christ. Once in a while, I manage to conquer my own hypocrisy and human weakness, and when I do so, I feel wonderfully close to God, and I know those are my rare moments of grace.

I 'm asking help from the Holy Spirit because only the spirit creates, and only the spirit illuminates a soul; alone one can do nothing. Sometimes my prayers are for myself, asking Him for wisdom, the wisdom to understand that His love is for all of us, deserving or non-deserving, nonbelievers or believers, Catholics, Protestants, Buddhists, Muslim or Jews. It took some time for me to accept this rationale, but finally I understood that nothing can separate us from the love of God, much less religion division. "The paradox of the Spirit is that we do not possess Him, rather that He possesses us, occupies us." But to enter into the peace of God, I believe one must pray and create his own oasis within.

Going into my backyard, standing under the orange tree, was the very beginning of my long journey into understanding forgiveness, love and peace. In communion with my private God, I also found the way to face and accept my human limitations and find the strength to deal with life challenges, like the acceptance of my little brother's death. Alvinho's death still hurts today, but I know that he and many others who died with AIDS, are in the city of God. They are in a place when as a child I was thought to call heavens or paradise. Today I call it the place where light, energy and absolute love exist, and where unity with God is the reality. Someone else said that God exists outside time; the past, present and future are all present to Him at once, and Jesus' sacrifice is always before Him. I believe this because grandma said that in paradise there is no time because time is a measure of change and there is no change in paradise. I realized that paradise is where God is, and hell is the opposite. Hell is God's absence, and for this reason I pray for God's mercy on me, a sinner. I ask forgiveness for leaving home and coming so far away to live on another continent, making my mother cry bitter tears for me.

I heard some people saying that AIDS was a curse from God, but I can't make myself believe that. I believe that every single death from AIDS is a tragedy, but it's not sent by God. It is a family loss and a calamity, it's maybe a curse, but not sent by God. Our loving God couldn't send it to us as a curse to punish His children. Jesus, when on earth, showed compassion and forgiveness. He came as the lamb of God; He came as the prince of peace. I believe He offered Himself for every single one of us, and His sacrifice was not in vain. He conquered evil on the third day. He victoriously went back to His father God Almighty with our debt paid off. This is my faith, this was taught to me by my grandma, and I believe nothing we do here can change this truth.

In some other dimension, they are together, Father, Son and Holy Spirit and with them vast legions of redeemed spirits that Jesus bought with his own blood. Today times are different, but the Spirit is the same, the same power, the same Holy Spirit, the same redeemer, our Lord Jesus. I remember one day when someone religious and righteous came to our home to visit our brother, and without compassion and full of ignorance, told him, "Do you know that God sent this disease to you as a punishment, and you now should repent?" My brother, with wisdom and humility, said to that person, "My God couldn't send this disease to anyone, not my God. He is a loving God; I couldn't love a God like yours."

Because of AIDS we suffered humiliation, we suffered prejudice, we suffered lack of support, and above all we suffered because there was nothing, we could do to alleviate our brother's suffering. Every moment with him was a moment of grace, it was a precious moment. We knew that in a short time he wasn't going to be with us anymore. Sometimes our pain was so real, so intense and profound that it became physical. I think what made AIDS the worst disease on earth was the absence of hope. A person can have cancer, or anything else, but there is always hope for survival. Not so with an AIDS patient. There was no hope for someone with AIDS. We knew there was no cure, there was no vaccination or treatment for AIDS in 1991. It was simply a death sentence. Now looking at my grandchildren, I pray to God above; to deliver our family and the world from this terrible disease and may we never suffer this agony again. May this never happen in our family again, not in our family nor any other family. May this tragedy never happen with anyone else. Our suffering was so intense that I believe it purified us all. I believe that God was among us during my brother's sickness. Only pure love could hold us together so tightly. I was glad that my grandma wasn't alive to see and participate in our sufferings.

With the knowledge that Alvinho had AIDS, our lives changed forever. Today, many years later, it's hard to believe that in different corners of this earth, every day someone will hurt the way we did, someone will despair the way I did, someone will cry to heaven the way we did in my family. Unfortunately, I know that every day it is happening again and again, in other families with other brothers. Even eighteen years later the death of my brother still hurts. My suffering has been transformed, but it has never stopped. Maybe that's why I couldn't write about him before, but with the passing of time I finally bring myself to do it. Dear Lord, I do miss him, I miss him terribly, and sometimes I catch myself thinking Alvinho would be so happy if he could be here. He would be crazy in love with his great nephews and niece. Alvinho, my little brother… AIDS stole you from us and what a great loss it is. One can transform grief but never eliminate it completely.

When in 1969 I married Bill, and came to the United States, I had no idea of how difficult the process of adaptation was going to be. It was extremely difficult for me to assimilate this new culture, to understand the language and to communicate with anybody. It was frustrating for me to deal with my daily mistakes, but I was learning the hard way. Many times, I cried, and I cried alone, hiding my feelings from my husband and from everybody in my family in Brazil. I tried to hide my failures and embarrassment by putting on a mask of bravery, but many times I felt miserable.

My first week in an English conversation class, my teacher asked me if I had seen any good American movies in Brazil. I told her in front of the class that I had: It was, "Three queers in the fountain". A second later the whole class came down laughing at me. I meant to say, "Three coins in the fountain". After the class had stopped laughing, the teacher told me, "Maria, please stay after class, I need to talk with you." I stayed and she told me what I had said and taught me the right word; it was coins and not queers in the fountain. Still, I couldn't understand her, then she again explained it to me, "What you said Maria, was three homosexuals in the fountain." After her explanation, I wanted to die, and it was hard for me to go back to class the next day, but I had to go back, because I knew I had to explain it to my husband, the reason why I was quitting the English class. I felt I was "between the cross and the spade" meaning that any way I was in trouble, or like my husband used to say, I was "between the rock and a hard place". But I remember my grandma Titida, saying, "Nobody is born knowing it all, one learns day by day."

Those days I needed a friend, but I had no one to help me, my help came from the Lord, I found a Catholic church and many days I went there and prayed. Many times, I prayed outside my home, my church was the universal church, it was under a tree looking at the sky that I converse with my God. It was under God's cathedral that I prayed the most, because everything down here on earth is sacred ground. But with the taste of bitter tears rolling down my face into my mouth, I promised myself that with God's help, I was going to make my life a success here in the United States of America. I had to be strong in order to fulfill my dream, because the price that I was paying was already too high. I knew that for many foreigners the USA had become the promised land, and for me it would be the promised land also. I started to rationalize that the early American immigrants had it hard too. They come from all parts of the world. They, too, had to struggle to adapt, some had suffered prejudice, and had sweated their own blood, but through it all they conquered a better life for themselves and created roots. They started new families and made new friends. With their hard work they made America what it is today, the leader among nations. I thought they were successful only because they believed in their dream, their strength had come from within, I was sure of that. They were ordinary people like me who had succeeded despite their own disadvantages. I could succeed too.

I had to believe in myself and in America, now my chosen country. I told myself I was going to make it my home; I was going to have a family and make my American children proud of me. Someday it would be us the Americans, no more of them and me.

As a new immigrant I was going to try my best for the good of my future American children and for the good of this country. I dried my tears, and told myself, from now on this is my country to live and to work and to die for if necessary. Someday I would graduate from an American university, I would become an attorney or a teacher because it was important for me to become a professional. I would show to my husband that I wasn't a bimbo from South America. I wasn't just a pretty face. My children would be proud of me. Someday, God willing, I would do just that.

It wasn't a dream; it was hope and desire to win in the game of life. What I needed was a good dose of humor and humility, to be able to laugh at my mistakes. My hope and determination would help my dreams become reality. I believe there's magic in believing. I was sure that I would achieve my goal. Behind me was Brazil, my family and friends and my unfinished studies at the University. I had left a completely different way of life. A new beginning was ahead of me and there was no turning back.

No one could know how difficult it was for me to live so far away from my little brother Alvinho and my grandma. My little brother was the love of my life, and only my God and I could really know how much I missed him. Leaving Alvinho behind was terribly hard because I had helped raise him. He was more like my own son than my brother. But I knew that I had to follow my destiny. I had made a choice and now I must go on and live my life.

Communication between my husband and me wasn't easy either. I remember one morning when he was asking me if I was though using the bathroom, using the bathroom. I didn't understand what he was saying. I heard him but didn't answer him. Having repeated the same question a few times, he opened the bathroom door, visibly upset. I told him, I don't understand what you are asking." He asked this time, 'Have you finished?' And I said, "Yes, excuse-me, I have finished, but I didn't understand the word 'through'." These little communication problems were the reason for friction between us. I know it annoyed my husband, but I couldn't help it. I was trying to learn the language as fast as I could. Many times, I felt like an idiot. It was sheer humiliation, and I cried bitter tears at those times.

I reminded myself that I came to America because I want to accomplish many things. I believed in the American Dream. I came to raise a family, to become a professional and help others accomplish their goals. I had to keep focused and I did. My dreams were waiting for the right time to become a reality. Because I believe. Later on in my life, I saw the results of my faith and hard work.

I stayed focused, I worked as a bank teller, and I saved as much as I could. Somehow inside me my desire to attend college was growing stronger. I wanted to live well, to take advantage of the educational system, to have a career, and make my children proud of me, a Brazilian immigrant. I want to say as Caesar said, "I came, I saw, I conquered." I wasn't going to be a 'blue collar' worker forever. I wanted more. I wanted my college degree, and I was going to get it. I wanted to teach the children of American immigrants. I believed that by doing this I would be able to pay back. I want to give back something that was going to help keep America strong. I knew that only through education could I accomplish this dream because like Vovo Titida always said, power was within, and I believed her.

I never doubted that someday I was going to enter an American university, and I was going to have my college degree. Inside me I never let this thought die. How I was going to accomplish my goal I didn't know because neither I nor my husband had any money saved to pay for my college tuition. I just knew that the Lord would provide, and in Him I trusted. Vovo Titida had said many times, "The Lord helps those who help themselves." I was ready to work hard, so prayers and hard work became my life. One day I heard a coworker at the bank telling another coworker, "Look whom the military boys overseas marry. I knew it was said for me to hear, but I said nothing and swallowed the insult. I knew this person wanted to humiliate me, but I didn't feel humiliated because I knew that I wasn't a loser. I just thought that this person was unkind and perhaps unhappy with her own life. Later that day I told my husband what I had heard, and he said that perhaps she was white trash, and then he explained the meaning of white trash. I counted the episode as one more lesson for me.

Sometimes I find myself asking these questions: why did I really decide to leave Natal? What forces inside me contributed to my decision to immigrate? Why did I want to leave Brazil, and not wait to finish school? My desire to escape from my father's house was strong. Was it my destiny? Do we have a destiny, or do we have free will? I was trying to blame my choices on destiny. I remember reading Escape from Freedom where Erich Fromm explained his theory about the individual fear of freedom. I asked myself, was I afraid of my free will? And is it possible that I didn't want to assume the responsibility of my choices because I was afraid?

Is this the reason why I say I had to follow my destiny? Perhaps, I really don't know. All I knew was that I wanted to leave home because I wasn't happy there with my father. I was young and restless, and crazy to be able to leave with the man I love. I knew Bill was the opposite of my father. Our children would call him Daddy.

. I liked Bill, was attracted to him. I told myself, if this fellow wants to marry me, I would say yes. I will leave college and go to the US. Once there I will finish my college. I didn't know how expensive college was or that my husband was not going to agree with my idea of me going to college. Things were very different when I arrived in the United States. I married Bill and discovered I had a hard road to travel.

Sometimes I think destiny played its part in making my decision because it was too much of a crazy thing to do, but I did it. In Natal people who didn't know me well called me Socorro, my friends and family called me "Co". My younger sister Fatima gave me the nickname, but when I came to the United States, I was called by my first name, Maria. It sounded so strange to me. I felt as if I had lost my identity but forty-two years later, I like the name Maria. It's simple, humble and it was my mother's name too. In Natal everybody called my mom Maria but her whole name was Maria das Gracas, (Mary of Graces). When I married my whole name was Maria do Perpetuo Socorro Cavalcante Menezes de Oliveira Clark. But when in Washington D. C. I had to go with my husband to the Pentagon, there at the door, the military man in charge of giving passes asked my name. My husband said to him,

"You will be sorry you asked." When I started telling him my name he said to me, "Please give me just the first and the last." He wrote Maria Clark, and it was as if I had been baptized again. From that day on I was Maria Clark to everyone, except my husband who still calls me by my nickname. Now my neighbors of thirty-nine years also call me "Co" and I like it. I like it when my husband calls me by my nickname because it makes me feel good. I feel as though I am the same young lady who he met at the ice cream parlor many, many years ago.

My marriage has not been easy. It's taken courage, renunciation, prayers, forgiveness and love to make it work, but today, forty two years later, I tell myself that finally I have arrived at a comfortable stage, no more tribulations in my life, this is it and from here only to eternity. Looking back…

In 1969 I left my home and came to the United States to marry Bill. When we arrived in Virginia, we found out that it was impossible for us to be married quickly in that state. Bill called his sister who lived in Las Vegas and she suggested that we could get married there right away. The problem was that we were both dead tired and flying for fourteen hours from Brazil. His sister had a friend who was a judge who would marry us the same day we arrived in Vegas. The reason Bill was so anxious to get married was because I told him that I wasn't going to sleep with him before getting married. By Virginia law we had to wait a few weeks before we could marry. He told me he wasn't going to wait a few weeks to be able to sleep with me. I told him that he had to because I wasn't going to sleep with him or anybody else before getting married. After that discussion I ran into the bathroom crying. I was terrorized: I thought that now I was completely in this man's hands and there wasn't much I could do. I went down on my shaking knees pleading to Saint Anthony to help me. I had left Brazil without my parents' blessings and now I thought I was going to be punished. After what felt like an eternity, I opened the bathroom door. Bill said that we were going to fly right away to Vegas to get married. He explained that we could wait a day or two and rest a little and that he was willing to wait for me until we got married. I told him that I wasn't tired at all, but I lied. I was dead tired. I was afraid that he wasn't going to wait any longer and would try again to make love to me. I thanked St Anthony in my heart for his help and immediately began packing my suitcase again. I remember when I opened the bathroom door shaking. I shook until I came in front of the judge in Vegas.

In Vegas, we went to his sister's home, and the next day we were in front of the Judge. When the Judge asked if I wanted to marry Bill, I was so nervous that I didn't say yes. His sister Magie told me to say, yes. I said yes, like if I were in a dream, I was so tired, so nervous, so worried. At least now I am married, I thought. Few weeks later I sent a copy of my marriage certificate to my father. My mom told me later, when dad received the copy of my marriage certificate. He cried for the first time in his life, she had never seen my Father cry. Few years later, when my daughter Moema was born, we went home to show the baby to my family.

After her birth, I thought I had created roots. I am part of this system; I'm an American by choice and I'm proud of it. Looking at the gorgeous sunsets of Tucson, I'm content, I feel great tranquility and I'm at peace. My second daughter Gina was born. Now they are mothers themselves, and I have three wonderful grandchildren. Rohwan, Asher and Riley. I have invested in my American family and now the dividends are wonderful, my grandchildren are clever and beautiful, Deo gratias! My little granddaughter Riley loves books. She is three years old and is already sitting in a corner for the longest time pretending to read a book. Sometimes the book is upside down, but it's cute watching her sitting there. I hope she will accomplish my last dream and grow up to become an attorney or a writer. As little as she is, she is already showing her love for books and signs of leadership. I hope she will become the writer in the family, the writer that I haven't become.

To be able to write was another one of my impossible dreams, perhaps the last impossible dream, to touch lives with my thoughts. I wanted my ideas to help people ask questions, make them think and be aware of issues. Inquire about some of life's mysteries or perhaps just make them laugh with some silly tales. But now all I want is to be able to open my soul the best way I can, letting my grandchildren and great grandchildren know me through my simple writing. But even to write my memories, I must have the talent to be able to communicate and have a profound knowledge of the English language. I know I lack both, and for these reasons I resign to humbly asking forgiveness because I'm writing these few memories. I want my grandchildren to know me from the time when I was a young girl named, "Co" and not this old lady who they learned to call Vovo. However, we have our plans, and the Lord has His. Who knows, someday my granddaughter Riley will do it for me. Before I close my eyes forever on this earth, God willing, I will see her writing for her Vovo. I wish I could see her becoming a successful writer. I must encourage her, show and guide her through the wonderful world of literature. This awesome world of ideas, just like my Vovo Titida did for me. I will try to plant in her little soul, the seed of faith and the hunger for knowledge. I hope to live to see my grandchildren grow up.

My younger daughter Gina, Riley's mother, married a young Mexican American man who did his graduate studies at Yale University, and in my daughter's words, my son-in-law Jerry, is a smart cookie. I'm sure our little Riley is a smart cookie too. Some day she may be a graduate from Yale just like her daddy did.

My daughter Moema married an Irish descent young man, and I have a mix of brown babies and white babies as grandchildren and I love it. Now I'm teaching them about God's children by asking them, "What color is God's skin?" And I am telling them that God has the color of love, He is brilliant as the sun, and his children are of all colors, just like the rainbow. Oh! This sweet wheel of life it's wonderful. Life is so wonderful! What a great gift from above.

''Thou know'st'tis common; all that live must die, Passing through nature to eternity" The Queen, in Hamlet.

Alvinho was ready to come into this world, and I remember as if it was yesterday. How excited we all were. Grandma held tight to her rosary, asking St. Anne, the mother of Virgin Mary, to protect my mother. Another of Grandma's spiritual duties was praying novenas to St. Anne, for protection of pregnant women in our neighborhood. They all came, some with boxes of votive candles for Grandma, some only asking her to pray for them. With my typical pragmatism, I remember asking her if she would pray the novena for the ladies who didn't bring her candles. She answered me saying that for these ladies she was going to pray harder because they probably didn't have money to buy candles. With my grandmother every day I learned something about life, she was a wise and compassionate woman. Finally, the time came for my mother to go to the hospital. This baby was the first baby to be born in a hospital; my sisters and I were born at the farm. My brother Bosco was born at our home in Natal.

    My mother told me how much she had suffered when I was born. (Mothers are like that sometimes. My mother thought like a good Jewish mother would think that a little guilt doesn't hurt anyone.) She told me I was born on the farm, in the hands of an old Indian woman, who was the only midwife on the farm. Soon after I was born the woman was giving me my first bath and was chewing tobacco at the same time. When she was done with my bath, she spat on my belly button. My mother screamed at her, but it was too late. My mom then got up from the bed and washed me all over again. The old Indian midwife didn't get angry at my mom, but she said that my mother was a white young thing who knew nothing about life. When my mother had finished with my bath, she gave her a gift for me. It was a snake rattle. She said it was to give me protection having been blessed by the medicine man. For some strange reason my mother kept the gift for a long time. I still remember playing with it when I was a young girl. It was kept in a small tin box, and I liked the sound it made when I shook it. It was my first toy and also my first encounter with mysticism.

After my birth my mother's life changed quite a bit in the following years. We had to leave the farm to follow my father to Natal, to live in the capital because of my father's new job with the government. My dad was going to work for the IRS, called "Departamento da Fazenda". Later on, my dad became the boss in this office and soon he was the head in the whole state; the Superintendente Fiscal. I remember my grandma telling us to pray for our father's soul because he had become a tax collector. From that day on every time, we prayed for the conversion of sinners, my dad was number one on the list. I guess my grandma was still making the connection with biblical times when tax collectors were considered some of the worst sinners.

Now my youngest brother was about to be born, and my mother was happy that she was going to have her baby in a hospital. When her time came, I went to the hospital with her as the oldest daughter. My father was traveling and not available. Grandma stayed home praying with my sisters.

That early sunny morning in August, Alvinho was born with his umbilical cord wrapped around his neck. When we saw him, he looked like a black baby. We all were surprised because he was so dark and our mother as a Portuguese descendent was white as snow. However, my father was a mix of Portuguese and Native American. My grandmother Anisia, his mom, was of Portuguese descent.

My grandfather was a descendant of the Tupi-Potiguar tribes. I remember grandpa never had a beard or mustache. His eyes were slanted almost like a Japanese person's. He was tall and handsome with a beautiful brown complexion. He also had a strong faith and a wonderful disposition towards life. I had great fun with my granddaddy. He was a happy and almost fearless man. He had a strong Catholic faith and a great love for God but was fearful of the powers of darkness. He believed that the religion of the Native Americans people in Brazil was mixed with strong powers. In

Brazil the people descended from Africans, had their own religion. Religion-spirit worship-was named Macumba and Candomble, and Grandpa was terrified of these religions. My grandpa never feared another man, but he did fear the enemy of souls more than anything else. He had great devotion to the Virgin Mary because he knew that Mary had conquered evil, and God had made her his first temple on earth. She was his powerful ally against the powers of darkness.

The slave descendants, who practiced their African religion in Brazil, made my grandpa extremely nervous. I believe it was because of his own background as a native American man who was raised with a great amount of superstition and mysticism. Somehow, he mixed his Catholic religion with his rich spiritual world, the world of his ancestors.

He was extremely different from my father: he was a happy man and very popular. He had the gift of gab and everybody in town loved and respected him. He wasn't the richest man in town but when he died, the people gave his name to the first high school: Escola Secondaria Olimpio Cordeiro. It was an honor for all of us. He was a cowboy because he owned a small ranch, but he also loved to work his land, planting all the vegetables needed for his household. Grandpa wasn't rich but had a successful small business. Nowadays one could call the store a small supermarket, but in his little hometown of Espirito Santo, it was called "Mercearia". He sold dry beans, cassava roots, potatoes and other produce from his farm. My grandpa was honest and a simple good fellow. He never went to college, but he sent my father because he valued education.

I remember visiting grandpa's house with my parents and having lots of fun. If our visits to grandpa were in June, the time for St. John Baptist's party, we would find a huge fire in honor of St. John Baptist in front of his house. He had cut the wood for the fire because he had also great devotion to St. John. June is the rainy season in Brazil and every time he tried to light the fire in front of the house, the rain came pouring down making his task difficult. He was always soaked in June's winter weather. He never gave up trying to keep the fire going. He would shout, "Viva St. John Baptist" from the terrace and we all responded, "Viva! Viva our Lord Jesus Christ, and his mother Mary, always virgin," and again our response, "Viva."

He kept the fire going until the late hours of night. He roasted corn and sweet potatoes in the fire, and we ate to our hearts content. He also kept fireworks going too. At the same time my grandma, Vovo Anisia, busied herself in the kitchen making cakes, cookies and other delicious treats for us. Vovo Anisia was a simple and humble woman. Her entire world revolved around my grandpa. Later on, I understood that she was trying her hardest to win my sisters' and my affection. We liked her a lot, but nobody could come close to our Vovo Titida who had always lived with us.

These were the days of my childhood, when I used to run barefoot after the blue butterflies and everything else that could fly at my grandpa's small ranch. At these times my feet and my sisters' feet and knees were always red, covered with a red medicine that we called "mercurio". I believe it was Mercurochrome because we always had cuts all over our feet and bruises on our knees. I remember one of my father's friends used to joke, "Everybody knows when you girls are coming from far away, because of the red Merthiolate on your bodies, you girls wear red from top to toes." Well, perhaps he was right, our mother was always cleaning the blood from our knees and toes, because my sisters and I seemed to run wild on the ranch wearing no shoes, going up into every mango tree, looking for the best mangoes to eat. We used to leave home in the morning only to come back in the late afternoon. We swam in the river, the Jacu River, and enjoyed every moment of our daily adventure. At home grandpa waited for us with a bowl of freshly cut sugar cane.

My mom's family came from the city of Porto in Portugal. Grandpa Jose, the Portuguese, died of tuberculosis when he was only thirty-five-years old, leaving my beloved Titida with a farm and four children to raise. My grandma Titida came from one of the best families of her time. She didn't hold a college degree, but she was extremely intelligent. She took care of her children, educated them the best way she could and left me with an un-measurable treasure, my faith. She planted the seed, and God gave me the grace to believe in Him today and until the day when I will see Him face to face.

Getting back to Alvinho's birth...

Well, our Alvinho was born looking like he was going to be a gorgeous dark baby. When the pediatrician came into the room, he explained to us why Alvinho was so dark. He had almost died at birth without oxygen because of the umbilical cord was around his neck. The doctor told us that he was going to be fine and, in a few days, his true color would show.

Just like the doctor had said, in a few weeks my brother showed his Portuguese blood. He had my mother's complexion. He was whiter than any of us and was just like our Portuguese grandmother. My father named him Antonio Alvaro. Because he had such a fair complexion, we nicknamed him Alvinho, which in Portuguese means, "little white". He was Alvinho to family and friends. When he grew up and became an attorney-in-law, my sister told him, now you must tell people to call you Dr. Alvaro, your nickname Alvinho doesn't sound proper for your profession. He told her, "I don't care, I like people calling me Alvinho. I'll show them that I'm a capable professional." He never allowed anybody to call him Dr. Alvaro. He was Alvinho to everybody. Today at his grave, on top of it there is a cross, and next to it only one name, ALVINHO, as simple and humble as he was.

We all adored Alvinho; he was our baby, our joy, our little baby doll. A month later after his birth, there was our Alvinho, with rosy cheeks, thick black hair and beautiful long hands. When my father saw him for the first time, he prophetically said, "These are the hands of a future doctor, these are the hands of a writer, he will be an attorney." In Brazil we call lawyers, doctors in law, and Alvinho grew up and fulfilled my father's prediction. He became Dr. Antonio Alvaro Cavalcante Menezes de Oliveira.

My sisters and I deeply loved Alvinho, as did everybody else who knew him. We all helped our mother take care of him. We also spoiled him. My mother thanked Heaven for her son. Her prayers to Almighty God had been answered one more time; she had her second boy. My father was very happy to have another son. He had three unwanted daughters and one more would be a disaster for my mom. It would be considered all her fault according to my dad. At that time in northeast Brazil, women were considered good wives if they worked in their kitchen, and obediently and blindly obeyed their husbands. In some homes husbands were the law and my home was no exception. In our house it was God, husband, kids and kitchen. In this order. Some husbands like my dad, would have liked it to be husband, God and kitchen because they thought they were mini gods. My grandmother Titida became a widow at thirty-five and was left with four children to raise by herself, but she never wanted to remarry. I remember her saying that her freedom was worth more than gold, and that she would never give another man the power to discipline her children or to control her life. She believed she had enough strength to be the disciplinarian of her children, and she became her children's father and mother. However, grandma's strength came from her faith in God. Her God was not a distant God and throughout my childhood I heard daily my grandma and my mom praising the Lord in our kitchen where they were working. Grandma would say, "Praise be to God our Lord Jesus Christ," and my mother would answer, "Forever be He praised."

Growing up God was always a constant presence in our lives. Our God was like our daily bread. He was essential; he was necessary for us to live as the air that we were breathing. He was real; he was a God of miracles, a Daddy, someone very close to reach. To me, my God was mother and father, I believed I felt that way because I had never been close to my daddy. Every night at bedtime our grandma sat waiting in our bedroom until we finished our prayers, asking for God's blessings. My sisters and I would say, "Bless me Daddy in heavens, bless me Mommy in heavens." Only then would we turn to Grandma and say, "Bless us Grandma." Every night we went to bed with the assurance that God was our Daddy, and Mary, Jesus' mother, was our Mommy in heaven and they were protecting us. The feeling of being loved and the peace that it brought to our minds helped us to quickly fall asleep. I believe it also helped us to grow up to be well-adjusted adults. Every night the routine was the same, after shower and snacks, we would listen to grandma's stories, and prayers would follow with the assurance of God's protection, and our dreams were peaceful ones.

Because of our grandma's love for us, we had a wonderful childhood. However, not everything was fun and good for my sisters and I, because in our home we lived with a devil called Lourdes. We had a young lady in our home, named Lourdes; she was our nanny and also our private demon.

Lourdes had come to our home to be my nanny when I was a baby. She was a black twelve-year-old girl. Her mother had died, and Lourdes lived with her older brother. My mother brought her home and loved her and trusted her completely. But unknowing to my mother, Lourdes' favorite sport was terrorizing us. Worse yet, she told my sisters and I about father's behavior with her. She told us he was sexually molesting her. Of course, we were confused and couldn't understand her stories completely. When she put my sisters to bed at night, she would scare them to death, threatening them if they didn't fall fast asleep. The few nights that they had our mother tucking them in bed, they loved it. At age seven, I was spared this torture because I went to sleep in my grandma's bedroom, my bed next to hers. But Lourdes, whom we all called Luda, always found a way to tell me about the same stories during the day. We all wished that Lourdes would somehow disappear from our lives, but our mother would always call Lourdes back to help, because my sisters wouldn't go to sleep soon enough for mom.

Some nights I went to my sister's bedroom to sleep there because we wanted to have some fun, but the moment we saw Lourdes coming in our bedroom, we settled down, making ourselves small in our beds, closing our eyes pretending to go to sleep. We did not want to listen to her stories about our father. We could not totally understand her tales, but we knew they were bad. Every night after giving us our baths, Lourdes would comb our hair pulling out hair hard enough to hurt us. Only my sisters and I knew how cruel she was towards us. I remember being spanked very hard, by my mother, because one day I ran after Lourdes saying, "I will kill this nigger, I will kill this nigger!"

I don't remember what she did to me, but I remember being spanked very hard, and then my mother putting me in her arms offering me to Jesus, for him to take me because she couldn't control my bad temper. At this time, I was little, four or five years old. Someone must have used the nigger word in the house because I learned it from somebody.

When I was seven or eight years old, I knew all about sex. Lourdes had instructed my sisters and me in the worst way possible.

Many afternoons at Siesta time, when my mom and dad had the bedroom room closed, she would call us telling us what my mother and father were doing at Siesta. Sometimes my younger sisters would ask me if what she was saying was true, and I remember saying no, she was lying and we all agreed that our mother and father wouldn't do such filthy things. Lourdes had described sex to us as nasty and ugly.

Lourdes' hate for my father was intense. She told us on a daily basis everything he did to her. She would tell us how my father behaved with her when she was alone. She told us that she couldn't take a shower without my dad looking at her or trying to look at her. She told us that father was always spying on her. Many of her conversations about our father's behavior we could not understand completely, but we knew it was not good. Today I understood the hell that was her life in our home. My father verbally, physically and sexually abused her. Not long ago I tried a conversation about Lourdes with my sister, who is now 62 years old, and she couldn't handle it, she asked me to stop and not mention her name and my father's name again. My sister is still in shame and pain because of what happened years ago. Lourdes was manipulative and mean to us. I believe she made everyone pay for what my father was doing to her. Lourdes, the oppressed, became also the oppressor. Today I understand what she went through and feel sorry for her, for the horror that her life must have been for twelve years. However, we were three innocent little girls, and she made us suffer for the sin of our father.

Finally, one day, our grandma told my mother in front of us, that Lourdes had to leave our home and go back to live with her brother. I couldn't believe my ears; we finally were going to get rid of our nanny. I was twelve at the time. Grandmother probably saw something happening between Lourdes and my father to take such a stance. My mother cried and protested. Lourdes cried too, but she wasn't saying much, and grandma was firm in her decision. I saw my mother crying for many days after Lourdes had left. Before Lourdes left, Grandma took her to a gynecologist and when Lourdes came back from the doctor she was crying. I saw her crying that day like I had never seen before. Later she told me that my grandmother had taken her to a doctor to verify that she was still a virgin and that the doctor had told her she was a virgin. She also tried to put us against our grandmother, but we knew that grandma loved us too much, and we didn't believe a word that she said. A week later when Lourdes' brother came and picked her up, my father was traveling and grandma said it was for the best. My mother was amazed why none of us had cried when Lourdes left, but how could we? Finally, we were free from her manipulative ways, no more from pulling out hair, no more threats, no more horrible stories.

A few days after Lourdes had left, we finally got the nerve to tell our mother why we didn't miss Lourdes. We waited before talking to mother because we wanted to make sure that she wasn't coming back to hurt us. We told everything that she had done to us, all her threats, and what she had told us about our father's behavior towards her.

Mother's face transformed into a mask of horror. Mother's love for Lourdes turned into mixed feelings, perhaps anger, pity and sadness. I saw my mother crying bitter tears telling my grandma, "I loved her, I loved her as my own daughter. "After Lourdes left, my mother told me that we were the only reason she stayed with my father. Quickly we saw our happy mother turn into a sad, unhappy person. She had a beautiful voice, and she liked to sing in the mornings but after Lourdes left, my mother never sang again.

Lourdes was twenty-four years old, and she had lived her adolescent years in a terrible hell caused by our father. She also pulled us all into her miserable life. She let us know about her horrible nightmare, and in doing so, she robbed us of our innocence and made us scared to death of our father.

Later on in life, when I was an adolescent, I understood and realized that the man who was my father, had molested a minor. I believe that this horrible family secret damaged all of us; our whole family became victims of my father's action. It affected each one of us in a terrible negative way. It left scars in our minds, our hearts and our souls. After Lourdes had left, nobody mentioned her name again. It was as if she had never existed. I had the feeling that Lourdes didn't like me because many times when I had affectionately called her Luda, she was rude and nasty. I grew up feeling ashamed and confused about the whole situation. I could never feel close to my father, none of us girls did. I remember one day, him telling my mother, "My daughters don't love me." It wasn't so much a lack of love, but we were terrified of him. He ruined Lourdes' life, but she ruined our relationship with him for life. Perhaps this was her revenge against him, but we were innocent of this horrendous crime of our father.

We were told by our grandma to love and honor our father and mother, that it was God's law, but we couldn't understand the wrong that our father was doing. How could we love and trust him? We lived in a permanent conflict with our conscience; we couldn't understand what was happening and why. Finally, today I can pray for my father's soul. I like to think that he was a sick man, I feel better this way, but it doesn't redeem him from his crime. May the Lord have mercy in his soul and in Lourdes' soul, who was a victim but also a tyrant.

That situation was a no win situation; we were all victims. I don't understand why we have so many evils on this earth, sometimes I don't understand why some people are so good, and others so bad, causing so much hurt to others. Many times, I have tried and wanted to wash away all these memories. I wanted them to go away. I wanted to forget and make believe nothing like that existed. When I was little, I wanted to leave home and never come back, and sometimes I wanted another father. I wanted a normal father, one who I could freely love, hug and kiss, and be proud of him and call him daddy. But my father was different; he was never a daddy. He was someone who we feared.

Nevertheless, he was my father and there was nothing I could do to change it. I didn't like my reality because it wasn't pretty, my father had spoiled it for me, so I decided to pretend that nothing had happened, and that it was all Lourdes lies, but deep inside I knew she wasn't lying. Later on, when I became an adult and was taking courses at the University, I understood about mental illness. I understood that my father was mentally ill, because he was always depressed. I thought, it's better being ill, than a monster, may the Lord forgive me for telling on my father. I hope that he has by now redeemed himself, and that he finds forgiveness for his soul, because he is still my father. Lord says, Love and honor thy father, but it's a tall order for a scary girl to understand.

Now I can see my father's positive side. My father was an intellectual, a man with refined taste and a giving heart. He helped a lot of people who came to our house asking for food, clothes or money, and I respected and admired him for that.

Life is such a mysterious thing, and for this reason, I place my hands on God's hands and ask Him to hold me. I must become a child again and trust, I need to trust with the trust of an innocent child. Today when I think about God, I see Him as my father and my mother. Because I didn't have a loving father, it's hard for me to see God as a male figure. For me He is my creator, father and mother.

Oh Lord! How can we understand the mystery of your cross, the mystery of human suffering? Why do you need our tears running into You like the river waters running into the ocean? I believe that

You are aware of every tear drop, every pain, every suffering. What is helping me today in my suffering and hard times, is looking at the big picture, looking through my whole life, remembering times when the hand of God was there, must have been there, giving me the strength for me to keep going, to keep living with hope. It's my belief that God 's love was what made me resilient, that He never abandoned me, and all that love deserves love in return. it's only just that we give it back to Him. I know that I will be judge by how much I have loved, and this scares me, and that's why I say, Lord teach me how to love, I let Him know that I'm still learning. St. John of the Cross, wrote, "In the evening of life we shall be examined in love." I understand that I must be transformed into love, I must die to myself and let love live in me.

I realize today that my university degree, my home, my car, my job, my material things, are of no importance. Only one thing will come with me on my judgment day, only one thing will be important; how much did I love my God, family, friends and enemies here on earth. How much did I love the Lord? Am I ready to stand in front of You? Oh, if only I could learn how to love like You do. You know it's difficult, but you still ask this of us. I want to do it, but I need your help. "Right now, I don't understand why a God of love came down and suffered for us. Why the cross? Why was it necessary? Was it your plan from the beginning? I have too many questions, Lord. "Lord, I believe, forgive my unbelief." God let me see, not only the beauty of nature, the moon, the rivers, and the oceans, but help me see the beauty of your love in the eyes of your children. Let me see their soul reflected through their eyes, in the tears of a happy child or in the smile on the sad face of a venerable old woman. Help me understand the difference and understand it. Let me find acceptance. Give me a content heart and your peace will be my strong hold."

Even today my heart aches for the sins of my Father and I pray, "Lord, please heal my family tree, heal those who have passed from this life, also those who are walking with me now in this journey going home, and the generations who are coming after me, bless us Lord in this valley of tears. We are all imperfect, but we are your children and your covenant with us is forever, we are bound in Your eternal love. This is the rationale that gives me peace and hope." Lord, do not let our minds, our tongue and actions hurt anyone. Guard our minds, bodies and spirit. I thank you Lord for the gift of faith, because without it I don't know if I could handle the shame and the hurt that I had in my soul for so long. With You I find the strength to keep going, hoping, living and enjoying the song of the bird in the freshness of a spring morning. Give me a strong faith to continue to trust You even when I don't understand the reason for our suffering. You are mystery Lord, and we are part of your mystic body, we are mystic people too. Today I feel broken, Lord, please heal this broken spirit and strength in me the power of your love, until the day when we will meet face to face."

Looking back, I still suffer for my father's actions, and for my family's sins of omission, I now ask forgiveness, with a humble heart. However, looking at the pains of others who suffered the devastation of a tsunami, an earthquake, war, of social injustice, child abuse or oppression, my pain becomes small and insignificant. Perhaps like a drop of water in the ocean of human misery. My suffering is nothing compared with the suffering of others; I have been protected and blessed. But precisely because of our collective sufferings, I cry to the heavens to make me resilient and humble, and to give me a giving heart, a heart of love. I ask for your healing power Jesus. You came to heal and in healing us, you redeemed us with your loving power. You took the cross and made our misery yours, because only You can love with unconditional love. It is You who brings me hope, helping me not to take my eyes from You. Like the morning sun, you renew my soul and my spirit rejoices in

You. Let your spirit create and soar free and renew the hearts of your people, thus renewing the face of the earth. Today I want to thank you for the many good things in my life. I want to offer You a gift, but I find myself empty, because everything that I have comes from You. My life, my family, my children, my education, my health, everything in my life is a gift from You. I have nothing to offer you, even my faith is a gift, so I come with a humble spirit offering You my will, and my love. You gave me free will, and I am giving it back to You. Lord let Your will be done in me, and not my own. Keep me close to You, hold my hand because I'm weak and I'm afraid to fall.

Now, back to my grandmother, many nights after I returned from my friend's home, I found Grandma sitting on her bed with her rosary in her hands. I'm sure she is making a banquet for the souls in Purgatory. On these nights grandma was my accomplice. She used to wake me up in the middle of the night to hear my boyfriend serenade me. She loved to hear his guitar. I love the idea that he was playing and singing just for me.

I couldn't picture my grandma young and sexy. To me she was always my sweet, old and comfortable grandma. She was small and a little on the heavy side, just like a lovely grandmother should be. She was the only person who comforted me when I was sick or sad, or angry at something. Grandma told me all about Luis Melo's poetry. She preferred to call him Loulou, like the rest of his family. She told me she dated Loulou before meeting my grandfather. This was Grandma's explanation to me. I asked her where she met Loulou. She told me they saw each other for the first time at one of the big balls at her uncle's house, and it was love at first sight. She'd been a skinny girl of sixteen, with beautiful red hair, blue eyes and an open heart waiting to be occupied by a prince or a poet. Loulou was there at the right time the night of the ball, just waiting for her. She said he danced like an angel, and that he loved her red hair. At the time she saw Loulou, her hair was long, full and beautifully red and she said, "It was nothing like now, just this little braid of gray hair." That night, holding in her hands a few pieces of her long gray hair, she said that one of the worst diseases on earth was old age, only old fogies knew about it. She told me that when Loulou married he gave his first daughter grandma's name. My grandma's first name was Clotilde. Later on, when he met my grandma again, he told her that the reason he had named his first daughter Clotilde was because he wanted to have a Clotilde at home. This way he could say the sweet name Clotilde as many times as he wanted. When I asked grandma, "Why didn't you name your first-born son Luis?" She said, "Never! I would never have done such a thing; it wasn't the right thing to do. I named my son after his father, your grandfather, who was a good man. It was destiny that was a stepfather for us, but before we were separated by destiny, we felt the sweetness of true love. He had his reasons for naming his daughter after me, but I had to honor my husband, letting the past be in the past."

I knew she had loved Loulou very much and never completely forgot his poetry because after his death, she always prayed rosaries for his soul. I never heard grandma pray rosaries for my grandfather's soul. If she did, it was very private and she never told me about it, but she did pray lots of rosaries for Loulou. Perhaps Loulou was for grandma, like a refreshing breeze on a summer day. The memories reminded her of the sweet aroma of her youth. She saved the memories of Loulou and his poetry in a special compartment in her heart.

What a romantic my Vovo Titida was. I was happy that she shared her memories with me. I believe she loved Loulou until the day she died. My Vovo was a young lady at heart, and a person who passionately loved life. She died at a ripe age of ninety-two, but her heart never wrinkled. I believe she was forever twenty-one.

Her spirit was as fresh as a spring morning, and her heart was always full of love for life. The gift of faith never abandoned her because the Lord was her strength. For these reasons I ask the Lord to let me follow in her footsteps and let love, faith and hope be always with me, and let love fill my heart until my last day here on earth. I don't want any other sentiment in my heart but love.

Perhaps I reminded my grandmother of herself in her youth, with the difference of our color, of course: she was fair-skinned, and I was brown like my father. Physically we were very different, but spiritually we were kind, and good friends. I was a romantic young girl of sixteen, who loved poetry, as much as she did, and like her, I loved God, nature and life. She told me that she had danced at many family balls. She had danced like no one else, at parties in her family homes. She also told me that she was a beautiful redhead in her youth and was never without a dance partner because of her reputation for having golden feet. I believe that this grandma of mine also loved it like nobody else, because of what she told me about her romance with Loulou, her young poet.

Grandma told me that Grandpa had helped those in need and that he had being a good husband. I can imagine and compare Loulou as being her golden key and my grandfather her silver one. I understood her, to me Loulou was her youth dream, and grandfather was her reality. When I grew up, I asked a few of her old friends about Loulou's poetry but nobody knew about it, and by that time, my aunt Sinha Louisa had also passed away. It was a pity that his poetry was forever lost.

Today I wish I had shared my first kiss experience with Grandma. I believe she probably would have understood. However, at that time I thought it might be disrespectful on my part. Besides, I couldn't predict her reaction. It was too risky, so I told no one. In my heart I thanked Grandma for her help: always defending my boyfriend's serenades, always being on my side. I knew I had a powerful ally. Since I was a small girl, we were bonded in love forever. She was my guardian angel. I also regret not telling her all about Lourdes. Perhaps it was because Lourdes' threats were too powerful and I was too afraid. At seven a child is extremely vulnerable. With the passing of time the pain has been transformed.

To us God was merciful. This was how we felt about God, and it was all because of our grandma. She was a flame of faith. Early in our lives she planted the seed of faith in our little hearts, and from Grandma's flame, the spark of faith in us was ignited. Later when I read what Pope John XXIII had written, "Every believer in this world must become a spark of light," I smiled with gratitude to my God for giving me Grandmother, Vovo Titida, who by her example and her teachings, had done just that. She was the sparkle of light not only in our home, but also in our community. Grandma was my first theologian, my teacher, my bosom friend and my confidant. Vovo Titida taught me about the immeasurable love of Jesus for us.

Growing up I created a private Jesus: he was totally mine, and yet I knew that He could be totally Jesus for someone else. However, my Jesus was unique. Nobody could know the Jesus that I knew, and only He could know the true me. I became very comfortable with my Jesus. Grandmother had told us many stories about Him and Jesus became our trustful friend, someone who would never disappoint us. Every night we had to pray the rosary with our mother and Grandmother thanking Jesus for His gifts to us and for our daily bread. We always prayed for our father to be converted. I believe these prayers for Father's soul only made us more confused and afraid of him. With time we understood a little more.

Our prayers were directed to many causes but praying for the conversion of my father and for sinners were a must. After praying to the rosary it was our bedtime, and grandmother would tell us stories. The stories were about the New and the Old Testaments, our family, or some literature. Sometimes a story telling us how faithful our God was for those who trusted in Him.

She told us the story of two good friends and godfather who were farmers and neighbors. One man told the other, "Godfather, I just finished planting my crops, and my crops will do good this year with the help of the rain."

The other said, "Well, my godfather, I just finished planting too, and with God's help, I will have a good crop."

And the other one said, "With the good rain, godfather, with the help of a good rain." Vovo Titida said that the other man repeated, "godfather, with the Lord's help." The rains came and it rained little on the crops of the man who had trusted only on the rain, but it rained really well on the crops of the man who had put his trust on the Lord. At the end the man with faith had the best results. We listened to the story, and we learned that the Lord was Almighty and powerful.

Grandma told us many stories about herself, when she was young and pretty. She enjoyed telling us about the time when our family had wealth, and her cousin Joao Villarim was the vice governor in Belem do Para, in the Amazonia, when rubber was as valuable as gold. She loved the fact that her family had political power and social status. Sometimes she seems to me a paradox because she was a humble person herself.

Grandma said that the vice governor's mother, my grandma's aunt Cecilia, had the best of things coming from Europe, and Yaya Vilarim, her daughter, used to say that her future husband was safe in her father's vault. I believe that Grandma was the poor cousin, she married my grandfather who didn't have any fortune, but they were happy and had five children. Unfortunately, my grandfather died at age thirty-five, as for Cousin Yaya, she was never married.

Grandma used to say that Yaya's husband got stuck in her father's vault and never could get out. I remember Yaya coming to our house for dinner. She was tall, well dressed and very elegant, and she walked like a queen. In Yaya's honor, my mother would dress us in our best clothes, and the table was set with mom's best China. My dad used to complain about these elaborate dinners. He said that Yaya was only a spoiled old lady, not the queen of England. After every dinner party, Yaya would renew her promise to bequeath each of us a diamond ring. Behind her back, my father laughingly said, "Girls, don't wait for these diamond rings standing up, you will be tired." My mother didn't care about the rings because she said my dad was right; it was all empty promises. Still, she felt sorry for Yaya, a lonely old woman. She was part of our family, and it was the right thing to do to invite her to our home. So, the dinner parties continued until the day the Lord called Yaya home.

What else I remember about Yaya is not too nice. I remember a cruel thing I used to say about her. Every time I thought one of my sisters was acting selfish, I would yell at her, "Yaya, Yaya Villarim, you are as selfish as Yaya." None of us wanted to be called Yaya. I ask her forgiveness, because today I believe as Grandma did, that Yaya, was a poor and lonely old soul. However, she was also a grand lady. She had class and I admired Yaya's hairdo, jewelry, clothes and her general aura. The way she looked and carried herself was unique. She never raised her voice. When Yaya was talking with my mother or grandma, I used to try to listen, only to lose interest and get bored in a few minutes because Yaya's conversation was a long and boring line of complaints. Thanks to this classy lady, very early in my life I realized that money was not much: it was just a tool that we need sometimes. Because of Yaya, I associated happiness with inner wealth, which we all thought she was lacking. But Yaya had virtues; My father studied in Yaya's house. If it wasn't for her, our father perhaps never had finished his studies. She was just an eccentric lady who seemed to be a ghost from the past, living her own peculiar ways. When Yaya passed away, we found out that she had a nephew, and he inherited all of her treasures including the statue of Venus from Italy. It was one of the wonders of my childhood, and a solid gold ''Oratory'' a place for all her saints. Some of the wealthy ladies in town tried to buy her oratory, however, she never sold it.

Time passed, I was a young lady, and my brother Alvinho grew up a happy and strong boy, by now grandma was ready for Alvinho. She provided him with one of the primary needs of the human psycho, the need for God. She taught him how to pray and how to trust the Lord our God. He was her next audience, and she did exactly the same as she had done with us girls, teaching him, loving him and telling him her wonderful stories. She also gave him all her love and attention. She took care of him the same way that she had taken care of my sisters and me. Alvinho adored her, and like us, he felt that she could cure all his ills, and that she could heal not only his body but also his soul. We believed grandma Titida was all-powerful and had a direct connection with God. We were lucky to have her as our own grandma. One year, I was already in Tucson, it was St John's Day. My family had a fire in our backyard. My brother Alvinho came close and told Grandma, my sisters and all the people who were next to the fire, including him. "I only believe that Saint John has power, if he sends a rain of fire. "My sister told me that as soon as he closed his mouth, the fire blew a rain of fire all over the backyard. It could be a coincidence, however there was wind. For everyone to see. It was St. John's miracle. My brother became white as snow, seeing this. How much I missed my family, no one else knows.

As time goes by, I manage to remember all grandma's stories because I kept them in a special place in my heart. Now I'm trying to do as she told me to do, walk the narrow path because it will take me to the Lord, and believe that the easy way, the larger path, takes us nowhere. Keeping her principles of Christianity, I try to hurt no one and to help everyone who is in need of something. Now that I'm a grandma, I'm trying to follow my grandma's steps but I'm coming up short changed because I don't have half her charisma or strength. In my attempt to become like her, perhaps I will be able to be half of the grandma who she was. I'm already telling some of my grandma's stories to my five-year-old grandson, Rohwan. I hope that someday he will remember a little of me, finding in his heart the seed of faith and the love for God and mankind, planted by me. If I can accomplish this, I will die happy. I understand that I'm planting the seed of faith in my grandchildren, but only God will make it grow with his grace. I try to love my grandchildren unconditionally as my grandmother loved me. I believe it made all the difference in my life because she provided us all with the necessary tools to become responsible and stable adults. Among many tools she taught us, the most important was love. "My land has palm trees where Sabia sings. the birds that sing here don't sing like the birds who sings there"

The Brazilian poet who was in Portugal, once said, "My country has birds singing, like the old Sabia, the birds who sing here don't sing like there".

I grew up in a traditional Brazilian family, father, mother, grandmother, sisters and brother, uncles, aunts and cousins. Sometimes an aunt or cousin would stay in our home for a few weeks. Friends in need were also welcome. It was a normal thing to do, to welcome family and friends in our home because in my culture close friends become family aggregates. Many relatives came to our home because they lived in the interior and they needed to see a doctor, dentist or to go to the hospital in Natal, the capital where they had better resources. Because they were all our poor relations, our home became their place to stay. My dad wasn't very happy with this situation, but we all loved the company. Sometimes we had six or eight relatives staying with us. At these times my father used to complain, saying that our home had turned into a free hotel for relatives.

We loved to have them in our home, especially at bedtime when we had to share our beds. To accommodate them all, we sometimes had to put two beds together and also had two or three hammocks going over our beds for our cousins to sleep in. Those nights we talked until midnight. It was a big and wonderful slumber party. Another peculiar thing was our chamber pot; it was white and had beautiful painted flowers on it. It was always under Vovo Titida's bed and it was for everybody to use because we didn't have a bathroom close by. The bathroom was outside in the backyard, and we were all afraid to go use it at night. In the morning Vovo Titida was the one who emptied it in the bathroom. Only now can I see what an unpleasant job it must have been for her, but she never said anything about it. Lord, I can't believe that we were all happy with the situation. I can't imagine my American daughters accepting their cousins sleeping in their bedroom in these conditions, what a cultural shock. I was sleeping with Vovo Titida in her bedroom all the time and I wouldn't change it for anything.

When my mother was busy making herself a wonderful hostess, supervising the kitchen, talking and gracefully smiling at our guests, my father sat in his favorite chair, keeping his face buried in a book, totally ignoring what was going around him. I guess that was the way he coped with the somewhat chaotic situation.

My father kept a constant distance between him and us. There was a wall of fear between us girls and my father. This invisible wall unfortunately separated us for a lifetime. When my father was around, we were three miserable scared little girls and yet Father never really spanked us or did any physical punishment. But he was so strict with us that a stern look from him was all that took to send us into panic or tears.

My dad was also a ladies' man and my mother knew about it but there was nothing that she could do about it. She had five children and didn't have a college degree in order to hold a good job. The best thing for her to do was to ignore the situation, pretend that she wasn't smart enough to understand what was going on. In front of everybody she always pretended she didn't know about my father's extramarital affairs. Sometimes I hear relatives talk about my father's love adventures and call my mom a fool behind her back. She never said a word against him to anyone, and to the bitter end, she was always at his side. How she did it, I don't know. When he finally passed away, she told me that if the Lord hadn't called father home, she was the one who would die. She had no more strength; she was exhausted. She had been at his bedside for all the fourteen years he was sick. My father had a male nurse night and day, but he wanted mom all the time.

When father became severely depressed and had a nervous breakdown, he was sent to a mental hospital for a few months. He lived for the next fourteen years at home suffering from depression. He took strong medication, but nothing seemed to help. We had to hire a private male nurse to help my father, and he lived at our house until father passed away. We considered him part of the family. After Father died, my mom found a good job for this nurse, and he stayed in touch with us for many years. My mother was sleeping in the same bedroom as father and Seu Jose, his nurse, but throughout the night my father called for my mother. He called for her night and day. I don't know how she managed the demand, because it would drive me insane.

I don't think Father was a handsome man, however, he dressed well. He always wore white linen suits. Sometimes he wore his Panama hat. His fingers were always well manicured, and he loved to wear the best colognes. He also loved good wine, a man of excellent taste. He was a refined man of his time. He loved literature with passion, and he was always reading a book or writing something. Most of the time he wrote poetry, and it puzzled me. To me he was a paradox: a man who never showed any sensitivity towards his daughters, any love. Yet he considered himself a poet. I could never see his sensitive side. He smoked a lot and consequently died with respiratory problems caused by his cigarette habit. He was seventy-two years old when he died. To my surprise I cried and realized that in spite of everything, I loved him, we all loved him. He was our father, but we hated many things about him. All my life I have been thinking that I never cared for him, but years later when I found out that he had a stroke and was blind in one eye, I cried and also felt pity for him. At the time of his death, I had learned to understand and separate his behavior from the father figure. When I was a little girl, I wished many times for a magic eraser to erase Lourdes, our nanny, and what my father had done to her from my memory. Today I never think about her, she is gone from my life, from my memory. Only by writing these memories do I remember the shame and the hurt.

Sometimes I admire my father because he helped people in need. He never denied help to people who had come to our home asking him for something. He never loaned money for a friend in need. Instead, he always gave it to them. He said that this way he was sure to keep a friend, otherwise, he would lose his money and his friend too. When I found out that he could read no more I hurt him. I couldn't imagine my father without a book in his hands. I owe my love for literature, the taste for the good things in life, and the hunger for learning, to him and my grandma.

From my grandmother I also inherited the love of books, she was always reading and sometimes she asked my mom or me to read for her. It was my faith, the most important element in my life.

My faith and generosity towards others I learned from her. She taught me that because we received freely from the Lord's bounty we also should give freely. I also believe that my passionate spirit I inherited from her. She loved life with passion and saw the beauty and goodness of the Lord in just about everything on this earth. She counted her blessings. With Vovo Titida, only the pluses counted, she was a happy person. Grandma used to say that we should be like a river, its water renewing itself every second, never looking back, never looking too much into the future, but enjoying the present moment. The only thing that wouldn't change in life was change itself, because change was a way the Lord had created to measure time. Grandma believed that in the heavens there was no change, and consequently no need for time. Heaven for grandma was communion with God, energy and light, eternal bliss and happiness. However, she taught me to be aware of the enemy of souls. She said he was a tricky one, but if we kept God's love within, we should not fear him. The Lord had given us a guardian angel who was always present protecting us. The only time that he could leave us was if we had committed a serious sin. She told me God was someone greater than our minds could comprehend, and any image of God was just that, an image, because He was infinitely more than we could possibly imagine. She taught us that we should learn to live the moment intensely because that moment would never be repeated, life was constantly changing. Our hands should be open. As soon as we were received from the Lord, we should give it to those in need. God gave good things to us because we needed not because we deserved, and for this reason we should give with a happy heart or receive with a happy heart.

Because I saw my father help people in need, I believe that he now sees the Lord face to face and is now one in the Lord. I hope his sins are all forgiven through his suffering here on earth. I hope that he repented before dying. Mother said to me that he suffered intensely before his passing, and went through his Calvary resigned with his suffering, accepting God's will. He never complained about his pains, accepting what was happening to him. For him I say this prayer, "Lord, don't look at his sins, but look at his sufferings, Lord have mercy on his soul." I also pray for Lourdes, asking the Lord to heal our physical and emotional hurting, hers and ours.

Sometimes I am terrified by the thought that my daughters or grandkids will pay for the sins of my father. Because of my obsession with child abuse, my sister advised me to do psychoanalysis, but only after my husband passway, I start going to one. I saw this doctor for 10 years. Now I'm trying not to bring that part of my childhood into my conscious mind because I want to admit that this really did happen and then forget all about it. However, now I know that my mistrust toward men comes from my traumatic childhood. I remember my mother saying that men were like dogs. Dogs could be holding a piece of meat, but if we threw a bone, they would pick it up. I guess she was referring to my father's infidelity. She was bitter because of Father's behavior.

When I was younger, things seemed easier: black or white, bad or good. When I grew up life became very complex making it difficult for me to understand some situations or make the right judgment. Unfortunately for me, I couldn't forget my father's sin. I kept it in my unconscious mind, and I carried my youth experience into my marriage. Even today I'm always worried about the safety of children. I feel like I can't let my guard down. I'm always on the alert, trying to protect my grandchildren. I wish I could feel less afraid for their safety. My father was also a complex man, someone whom I admired and feared at the same time. From the time I was a little girl I had known his darker sin. But God heals our bodies and souls. Through His mercy and love, today I feel that I'm whole. I am happy and at peace, but it was a bumpy, long journey to be able to forgive my father. I will never completely forgive myself for what I did with my husband and children. I just pray that we don't pay for the sins of our fathers. looking at my life and counting my blessings, I know that the God Almighty gave me more blessings than I deserved. "Bless the Lord, O my soul, bless His holy name, all that is in me!" Psalm 103

More About Alvinho

Our brother Alvinho was our gift from God. He was a bright child, learning everything very quickly. I loved him like my own son. He was a very active little boy. When he was two years old, he burned his little feet in the kitchen. It was a stupid accident. We were all in the kitchen at that time. A pot of boiling water was on the stove, when suddenly we heard the scream. Alvinho had pulled the pot of boiling water all over his little feet. Thanks be to God; it was not on his face or body. I ran with him in my arms to the neighbor, and we took him to the hospital. It was sheer agony for both of us. He held tightly to me, crying all the way. I believe that emotionally I was hurting more than he was because there was nothing, I could do to absorb his physical pain. That was the first time I felt my brother's pain. I wanted to feel and suffer for him. I wanted to take his pain away, but I couldn't. I felt and knew then my profound limitation. As a child Alvinho had such deep belief in me, and I felt that I was letting him down. I couldn't work a miracle, the miracle that perhaps he thought I should do. Thanks to God, Alvinho recuperated quickly and without bad burn scars on his feet. Soon he was running around the house making everyone smile at his little games.

My Alvinho was seven when I left home. It was totally my choice; The truth is I didn't realize the total impact of my decision. I was living behind my family, college, friends, culture, religion and country. I was leaving my life behind me. I was embracing a whole new way of life and leaving my comfort zone. It scared me and many times I thought of telling Bill that the deal was off. For some reason I never did. I went through with the plans to marry him and immigrate. I tried not to think too much about the situation and waited for things to happen. I believe that if I had thought a little more, I wouldn't have had the nerve to leave. In Brazil people used to say, "He who thinks, doesn't marry, and he who marries, doesn't think."

Today I ask myself, how could I have done that? Was it really my destiny? I always believed that we make our own destiny, I also believed in a certain amount of freedom given to us by God, to choose our own path, and yet I wasn't so sure about anything anymore. I let myself make a serious decision without analyzing myself thoroughly. Part of me wanted to go and part wanted to stay. I decided to gamble with my life and told myself it's now or never. But with my freewill I was choosing to come to the United States. It would become my country by choice, and I was going to know America and I was sure that I was going to learn how to love it.

But Brazil would always be my beloved land. Brazil would always be in my heart. When the time to leave came I knew it was my choice, and my own responsibility. No one else had influenced me to leave. I had no idea of the long and hard road that I had in front of me. I left Brazil because of my father. I was rebellious towards his xenophobia. I remember finding little pieces of papers all over his desk or inside a book that he was reading saying 'I am xenophobic'. I knew it was there for me to find. It was my father's way to let me know that he didn't approve of my marriage to a foreigner. I never confronted my father about it. I never had the courage to say much to him, but I knew that he wasn't happy with my choice.

It's one thing to come to the United States looking for survival; it's another to come because of an ideal or to escape a situation. Nevertheless, whatever the reason, it is a hard decision to make.

But I think that leaving everything behind, leaving all my good chances in my own country to embrace an adventure and a different life in a foreign land was harder and it was crazy. Only a young person could do such a thing. And it seems to me now that I was trying to escape something that was deeply rooted inside me.

I soon found out that I had brought with me all the ghosts of my past and nothing much had changed because what I had inside me I brought to America. My bad memories didn't go away but I was happy to be able to move away from home. I didn't hate my father; I only disliked his behavior and feared him. Many times, I caught myself asking if there was such a thing as karma, and if there was something like a frame, or a path where one must follow. Soon I found out that life doesn't give many answers. We have to learn how to play the game one day at a time, one way or the other, we could come out as a winner or a loser. But I wanted to play to win, and I didn't want the role of victim. In the deepest place in my soul, I had the desire to finish college in this new country. I wouldn't share this dream with anyone because I didn't want people to laugh at me. My husband didn't have the money to send me to a university; besides, he didn't even support my ideas or share my dreams. Once he asked me if I had come to the United States only to go to college or if it was because I loved him. My answer to him was, "Hello, I was in college in my country, it's obvious that I want to finish college here in the US and this has nothing to do if I'm in love with you or not." So, college at the moment was my impossible dream, but in some place in my mind I kept my dream alive, never letting it die. Every time I passed close to the University of Arizona, I said to my mind, heart and soul, "Someday I will be here studying. I may not become an attorney, but I will be here, I will have my degree." I wanted that with every fiber of my being. My husband was totally against the idea of me going back to college, and for this reason he paid for a secretarial school for me. He said that becoming a secretary was a good job for me. I agreed that it was a good job, but not for me, because I had a dream and my dream was going to become a reality. I believe that if you want something and visualize it, it will become a reality.

In 1976, Alvinho was sixteen and a senior in high school. At that time my father was very ill, suffering with depression and emphysema. My mother and my sister asked me to bring Alvinho to my home here in the United States to study English for a year. They were concerned about his health as he was a sensitive boy, and my father's condition was having a terrible effect on him. He was sad most of the time and my mom was afraid for his mental health because he was becoming a different boy. He was losing the joy of life and the interest in his studies. Immediately I talked with my neighbor, Tom Anderson, who was an attorney, and Tom made arrangements for me to become Alvinho's tutor.

Alvinho flew to Phoenix where my husband and I went to pick him up. I had not seen him for almost two years, and when I saw my brother, he was a tall skinny fellow, not my little boy anymore. I hugged him and said, "Alvinho, you are so skinny." and he said, "And you, Co, are so fat, how did it happen?" I was almost nine months pregnant with my second daughter Gina. We laughed and he told me that when he left the plane and walked towards the airport, he thought he had landed in hell and not in Arizona. It was August and the middle of a hot and humid summer. I told him that in Tucson the weather was a lot better, and that I believed it was in Phoenix at summertime that the devil had lost his boots. We were so happy to see each other. He kept saying everything is so barren, where are the trees? I told him that this was the desert land of Arizona and not tropical Brazil. I told him that he was going to learn how to love it like I had done, and I was going to show him some spectacular sunsets and sunrises. A few days later we took him to see Mount Lemmon near our home and a beautiful place to cool off a bit from the implacable desert summer. Alvinho loved the trip to Mount Lemmon and it became one of his favorite places.

Alvinho was a senior in a private school in Brazil, so we enrolled him in a private school. But he hated this private school here and asked me to put him in a public school. My family had paid tuition for a year at his private school, and our neighbor Tom, the attorney, helped us with the necessary papers to receive half of the tuition money back from the private school. We had to pay the state for Alvinho's half year at Sabino High School. I tried to argue with the superintendent of District 1. I told him that we were taxpayers and my brother was going to stay only six months at Sabino High. However, he was inflexible in his decision, and I had to pay tuition for my brother to study at Sabino High. It seems ironic that years later when I became a teacher at District 1, and Sunnyside High School, I taught many undocumented immigrants who never paid tuition.

Alvinho loved the US. He thought school was easier here. He made friends, went to parties, gave parties and received his friends in our home. I believe he had a good time and his stay here was of great value to his education.

I was pregnant with my second daughter Gina, at the end of January 1977, when my sister called from Brazil telling me that Grandma was very ill, and that she had gone to the hospital. I felt sorry for my Vovo Titida, because I knew that she didn't want to go to a hospital, but everybody told her it was going to be better if she went. She had had a thrombosis, what I think is something like a stroke. My sister later told me that when Vovo Titida was getting into the ambulance, she waved to my sister, saying good-bye and my sister knew that she wasn't coming back home. I was very pregnant with Gina. Alvinho was staying with us, and I couldn't leave him with my husband and with my daughter Moema, who was one year old. We were very sad with the news, and somehow, I also knew that Grandma wasn't coming back home. She had never been sick before and I had a bad feeling about the situation. A few weeks later we received a phone call from Brazil letting us know that our grandmother had passed away; she was ninety-two years young, because her spirit was young and her mind was sharp as if she was only twenty something. We were devastated by the news of her passing. I was numb. I knew that she was old, but I thought that I was going to see her one more time. We knew that she had had a thrombosis and was in hospital, but we didn't want to think the worst. At the time it was impossible for us to go to Brazil. Even if we had gone, by the time we arrived there, she would be buried already.

Alvinho adored grandma just like we all did. At first, I couldn't cry for my grandmother, I wish I could have, but I just had an awful feeling inside me. It's hard for me to describe it: I felt pain and a feeling of tremendous loss. I wanted to scream, to run, to cry, to do something, but I did nothing, something was tight in my heart. Later on, Alvinho and I cried together. We shared the pain knowing that it was the same pain, and when we cried, we felt better. Later I realized that our grandmother couldn't die completely because she would always be with us. I remembered her teachings, her rationale, her stories, her life, and I realized that she had become part of me and that part of me would never die. She was going to live with me as long as I lived and I would take her with me to eternity. I never cried much for my grandma, I just continue loving her and remembering her alive, and I will do that until the day I breathe my last breath. In my mind she isn't dead, she is living in a better place. When my second daughter Gina was born and I came home from the hospital with her, that same night, for the first time in my life, since her death, I dreamed about my grandmother, and it was a vivid dream. I saw her coming into my bedroom, and when she sat on my bed, she made the mattress give in with her weight. She was a little on the heavy side. I said to her, "Vovo Titida?" Because I was surprised to see her, then at this moment I opened my eyes. It was six o'clock in the morning, and I knew that I was dreaming, but this dream was very real. This was the first and the last time that I dreamed about her. I believe she came to visit my new daughter and me. It was more like a vision than a dream. I believe she came in spirit to visit my little baby girl and me.

Alvinho went back home after his year with us and had to repeat his senior year in high school because of some education law in Brazil. He was devastated because of that, but I told him he was very young, and that his year in the US was a valid and positive experience in his life. Finally, he accepted this setback, finished high school and took the exams to go into law school. He passed the examination for the first time. This exam is called the "Vestibular," from a Latin word meaning to enter. I was very proud of him. In our family, we were all proud of him. He was a handsome and refined young man, a gentleman and very diplomatic in his actions. Five years later our Alvinho became Dr. Antonio Alvaro, because in Brazil all attorneys in law are called doctors. However, he asked his clients and everybody else to just call him Alvinho. Only at the forum when he had audiences was he called Dr. Antonio Alvaro.

I was always very proud of my brother and his success in his career. He had worked for a travel agency during college, and after graduation, he worked with a friend of my father at his law firm. Life was good for him. After a few months in the law firm, Alvinho decided to study to become a judge. At this time, I was working at a local bank as a teller, but I had my goal, my secret goal to save enough money to pay for my college tuition. I hadn't yet had the chance to go to college in the US because it was too expensive. Few years had passed by, and my dream was still alive. I wanted to finish my college degree, and I was going to do it sooner or later.

I remember. One day I was visiting my family in Brazil when Alvinho asked me, (he always called me by my nickname), "Co, why don't you finish college now?"

"Are you kidding? I can give you a few good reasons why not, first because it's too expensive. Going to the College of Education isn't what I want to do. I want to have my Law degree.

Alvinho told me that I was intelligent, and that it was a pity that I wouldn't try because I could become a teacher or an attorney. I could become the professional I had always wanted to be. He also told me, "I listen to you when you advise me to choose a career, why don't you listen to me now?"

I said nothing more to him, and I know that he was disappointed. But inside me I said, "why not? Why don't I try it? All that I have to do is try it. I have nothing to lose, and this is one of my most secret dreams." I was reasoning with myself and getting the nerve to try to go back to college. Alvinho was only reminding me that I had a dream.

The AIDS Journey

It was sometime in 1990-January or February, I can't recall the exact month, but it was at the beginning of the year when I received the phone call that changed my somewhat peaceful life. I was working at the bank, in fact I was in the middle of my break, when a coworker told me, "Please, pick up the phone. It's for you from Brazil." Immediately my heart raced, and I felt cold; a strange chill took over my body. I knew it was trouble because my family had never called me at work. With shaking hands, I picked up the phone. It was my sister Fatima who said Alvinho wanted to talk to me. I knew something terrible had happened because I could sense something wrong by the tone of her voice. When he came to the phone his voice was breaking. "Alvinho, what's happened?"

He said, "Co, I went to the doctor, and he asked me to have an AIDS test. Please pray that the test comes negative." I couldn't believe my ears, then I said, "AIDS? The doctor must be joking, who is this doctor?"

"He is a very good physician and a friend of mine," Then he told me that this doctor was recommended by his girlfriend who was also a physician. I knew my brother well, and I knew that he was very worried. He was reaching out for me because he was afraid. I also knew that he loved parties, his favored party was Mardi Gras, in Salvador, in the state of Bahia. Carnaval, or Mardi Gras, was a synonym of excess. Immediately I thought about unsafe sex during Carnaval time. It was and still is the craziest and dangerous party in Brazil, especially in late years it turned out to be nothing less than a pagan orgy. However, when I was young it was different, nothing like nowadays. I had a lot of fun at Carnaval, probably keeping my guardian angel quite busy, because nothing bad ever happened to me at Mardi Gras' times. I asked Alvinho if he had ever had unprotected sex at Mardi Gras or at any other time? And his answer was no. He admitted that he had a little too much to drink, but he couldn't remember having unprotected sex. He assured me that he always had protected himself. I told him not to worry that the test would come out negative.

But I was also very worried, and that night I couldn't sleep. I kept thinking about clues, something that would tell me if he was gay. I couldn't find anything in his behavior that indicated he was a homosexual. I couldn't believe that my little brother was gay or bi-sexual, what to me was the same thing. I remember everybody in our family being prejudiced toward gay people, including myself. Then I thought about the anxiety and agony that probably had been with him all his life if he was gay; the tremendous effort to cover it up because he also was a product of our prejudices. He knew how the family thought. My heart ached for my little brother. He was probably afraid of rejection and feared discrimination among us. I had been intolerant with gay people and had made some negative comments. We all had been merciless and ignorant towards gays, and now a shadow of doubt was in my mind. The person who I loved most on this earth, could be gay. Alvinho had many friends, boys and girls. His actual girlfriend was a physician, a blonde girl, because he always had a preference for blondes. When he was living with me for a year, our neighbor had a daughter, a beautiful girl, named Kelly. Alvinho and Kelly were always together, day and night. They were both sixteen. When he was living here at my home in Tucson, there was no indication or clue that he was gay, we saw no signs, no red flag. I thought he was a handsome, healthy, and happy young man who was also sensitive and thoughtful of everybody. I remember grandma telling us the story of Sodom and Gomorrah, and how much the Lord had despised this sin, and that the word sodomy was because of the sins of Sodom and for this reason the Lord had the two cities destroyed. I didn't grow up calling homosexuals 'gays', this new label came years later, and we used pejorative words towards the homosexual community. It seems that it was the norm, and we never stopped to think that gays were human beings with the same needs as everybody else. Homosexual behavior was to us, an ugly and unaccepted behavior, a question of choice, a question of moral decadence. We were taught this as a Gospel truth, and my brother was also a product of our environment; he knew our rationale.

 The more I thought about this, the more I suffered in agony for my little brother. Oh Lord, my poor brother, my Alvinho, and immediately out of love for my brother, my aversion towards gay people began to disappear. I began asking questions and reading about the subject, a subject that I always had avoided. Now I was eager to understand the reason for this behavior. I wanted to see it beyond prejudice and discrimination I wanted to be fair and not judge before I could understand the behavior because a just God, as my God was, wasn't going to deny salvation to these people. I prayed for wisdom and understanding, and I cried bitter tears for my brother and for my family. AIDS in our brother was an unspeakable tragedy. I prayed to God, please Lord, make these tests come out negative.

Unfortunately, the tests were all positive and the second phone call from Brazil was more difficult. Thanks be to God; I was in the privacy of my home when the second call came. My brother was crying and asked me to come home. He had received the bad news from his doctor friend, and that the doctor had cried with him, before giving him his death sentence. He told me that when the doctor had asked him to do the AIDS test, he really never had expected that the test would be positive. At that time, I felt numb. I wanted to say something, but I didn't know what to say. I felt something cold going through my body, and I felt the most extraneous emotional pain. That moment was one of the most difficult in my life. When finally, I could talk, I told him that this test could be a mistake, they make mistakes at the laboratories. He said that he had taken another test and that too had come back positive. It was no mistake. This test was the third test, and it had been done in Sao Paulo in one of the best laboratories in the country. There was no mistake, and for him there was no hope. I felt my knees weakening and I had to sit down. At that moment my whole soul let out a silent scream, but my mouth was silent, silent for him. I thought of my mother, I knew her heart was now pierced, that she was mortally wounded because my brother was her baby, her pride and joy.

I knew my brother was sentenced to die soon. I couldn't accept this curse upon my brother; he was only thirty and looked so healthy and handsome. Anybody who saw him would see only a healthy- and good-looking young man, well groomed, well educated, a true gentleman and a winner. In 1990, nobody knew much about AIDS, only that it was a killer that there was no cure for, and only homosexuals got this disease. I told him that I was going to buy my ticket as soon as possible, and I would come home to be with him. He should try to have faith; some cure was going to happen.

After my conversation with Alvinho, I sat down to think about what I was going to do too. I was still feeling numb from the news. I was so numb that I wasn't able to think because I was in a state of shock. Later on, I called my travel agent and made the arrangements to fly home. I asked myself what was I going to do? How could I help? The only thing that I knew I could do was to be there for him, but I wanted to do more, much more. My feeling of impotence was overwhelming. I had no idea how much more suffering I was going to witness. Not only my brother's suffering at Calvary, but the suffering of those who were going to share his fate at the hospital and the suffering of my whole family.

I went home feeling totally powerless, knowing that I could do nothing to make my family or him feel better. The shadow of AIDS was too heavy on me to carry on. It pulled me down, and sadness became my daily companion. Sometimes I was profoundly sad and close to desperation, but I had a family of my own, my two young daughters needed me. For them I tried to fight my negative inner feelings and look for survival for me and for him. I knew I had to be strong, but dear Lord, how was I going to be able to stay strong for them?

When I went home for the third time I found Alvinho physically changed. He didn't look like the same person: he was debilitated, he was only skin and bones, but spiritually he was the same. He was a pleasant old person, even working at home. He asked our two married nieces, who had come from Switzerland, where they were living, and me to come with him to his office. The trip to his office was hard for Alvinho. He could hardly walk I helped him by embracing him on one side and my niece Moema, did the same on the other side. Even then he had no strength. When we reached the elevator, he said, "My God, it wasn't too long ago it was so easy for me to climb the stairs. I seldom used the elevator to come to the office." At his office he joked with the secretary, we all had a good laugh, and he rested a bit before leaving. We all knew that it was a tremendous effort for him to go to the office. It was too painful for us to see Alvinho in this condition. I don't know why, the more we love, the more we suffer. Someday I hope to understand this equation.

One day Alvinho told my sister he needed to see a friend to get out of the house. They went to Elisa's house, and her mother told them that Elisa wasn't home, but my sister saw the girl inside. They left, and he picked another friend's home to visit. The same thing happened, they tried another friend and for the third time, no friend was available, and nobody even invited them to come in, but there were people clearly there. My sister knew that nobody was going to open their doors for them. Alvinho also understood and told her they were afraid of AIDS, it's worse than leprosy. He said to my sister, "Don't cry Tata, let's go to God's house, His doors are always open." My sister asked him, "Are we going to church?" He said, "No, we're going to the beach, we're going to be under God's cathedral, the most beautiful one, the outdoors, with the wind, the music from the ocean and the blue skies. This beautiful earth is God's house. He invites us all to live in harmony and in love, in this beautiful world, but many people don't see its beauty, and don't get the message." My sister said that he turned on the radio in the car and started singing to the music. This was my brother; he had already forgiven them because he understood their fear, their ignorance and prejudice. He believed that God was Omnipotent; he knew that God could be at all places. Alvinho was never bitter, he never said, "Why me?" He was a warrior, a fighter, but he knew that it was going to be hard to win this last fight. However, he managed to have hope. He told me one day that the next year of 1993 would be a good year, a year for the discovery of a cure for AIDS. Unfortunately, it wasn't the way he thought. It was the year of his liberation, of his freedom from his earthly body, he was finally healed. He had been purified on earth by his terrible sufferings. We never knew what infection did kill our brother, but his stomach was swollen, and he suffered tremendous pain through his body. We suspected he had cancer in his intestines, but he never complained. He also had sores on his lower back, and my sister and my nieces took turns cleaning them.

In the beginning of his sickness Alvinho stayed at home. He was afraid of going into the hospital, but a time came when my sister called me and asked me to come home again. Alvinho had contracted a disease called toxoplasmosis, and it was very serious. When I went home a year had passed by and my brother wasn't the handsome, well groomed, young man he had been. He was only a shadow of what he once had been. He had lost control of his body functions; sometimes his feces ran down his legs, sometimes it was urine coming freely down his legs. Seeing my brother in that condition felt like someone had put a knife through my heart. I was not only crying for him but for all of us. I felt a tremendous pain inside me, almost as if it was physical. My mother and my sister felt the same way. We were united in this horrendous pain and suffering.

When I arrived home, I quickly made arrangements to take my brother to a hospital. I convinced him and took him to the Giselda Trigueiro Hospital, because otherwise he would have died quickly at home. I became a pragmatic person, the strong person that I wasn't, but I had to be because nobody else was at my home. Being strong for them was the only way to help my family. Nobody else was able to think clearly. I'm sure the Lord gave me the necessary strength because it was a miracle that I, too, didn't collapse in despair.

At the Giselda Trigueiro Hospital, the only hospital for AIDS patients in town, I saw children, young ladies and young men, all just waiting there, waiting for nothing, because they were there waiting only for their own death. The hospital didn't have medicine or food for the patients. It lacked all the necessary supplies to help its patients. The AIDS patients went to Giselda Trigueiro Hospital with some hope, only to find out that there, or anyplace else, there was no hope. It was hard, very hard, to see them dying without hope. There were no medicine and no support from a group, nor did they have psychologists available for them. The stigma of AIDS was so great that no one wanted to get close to the area reserved for the AIDS patients. I saw a young man, an AIDS patient in need of surgery. Some doctors were afraid to operate on him. I don't know if that man ever got the needed surgery. People in the AIDS ward had become untouchables. It was tragic to see my loving.

brother on death row, and worse yet, to feel fearful of catching his disease. I couldn't show my fears to anyone or admit them. I had to be there for my brother, but I thought about my daughters, my husband, my family back in the United States, and I said to my Lord, "Protect me dear God, because I'm going to do what I have to do." I stayed helping my little brother until the end. His suffering was unbearable to see, and yet I had to be strong for him. I had to be there with my family, we had to hold on together, alone we wouldn't stand. Looking around me, I start thinking about the purpose of life. I started questioning: who are we, what are we doing on this earth, why, why, why, why, so much suffering? And I felt just like an empty boat being carried down by the currents, empty of almost everything, but most of all, empty of hope. No direction, just going where the wind would take me. For my companion I had my pain, my profound hurt. There were days when my sister Fatima felt worse than I. Sometimes coming from the hospital, she would cry and scream, "No, it's not true Alvinho doesn't have AIDS. I'm losing my mind." I held her and would say, "Yes, it's true, our brother has AIDS. We are going to be together and be calm for him; we do not need another tragedy. You can handle this. We are together, we will have the strength, he needs us, and we will be strong and healthy for him. Stop this behavior." At these times I was afraid that she would lose her mind. Going through this all, I felt closer to God than ever, but I couldn't pray, nobody could. I offered our sufferings as prayer to God, and I knew that only the grace of God was giving us courage. I never thought I had to be so strong, or pretend to be, but I knew everybody was looking at me as if I could work a miracle, Oh! Dear Lord if only I could. I felt so impotent; there was nothing I could do but just be there for them. Lord Jesus after the tragedy of AIDS, in our home, nobody ever could be the same. It changed all of us.

At times I caught myself thinking that just a few weeks ago, Alvinho seemed healthy, full of love for life, and with plans to become a brilliant judge. Now AIDS has destroyed every dream, every chance of a future, every chance of life, and my brother knew this. I tried to feel like him, I tried to understand what could be going into his mind. The only feeling I could have was sadness. I couldn't walk in his shoes, I couldn't feel what he was feeling, nor could I feel his pain. I could only be there for him. However, I understood how fearful he was; death, this old monster, was closing its circle, and he knew it. There was nothing I could do to alleviate his suffering. His reality was terrifying. I could only suffer with him, be there for him and pray to God for mercy. I could do nothing to send the hearse away. I knew how much he feared death because I knew how much he celebrated life.

I went home and this time the neighbors didn't want our family to stay in the neighborhood because they were afraid of the disease. People avoided stepping on our sidewalk, and someone put some voodoo stuff on our porch to scare us. I realized that we couldn't stay in our house, not because of the voodoo threatening, but because the people were afraid of us. I was afraid of them too. At that time, no one knew much about Aids. Today it was the voodoo on our porch, but what about tomorrow? What else would they do to us? We had lived in this neighborhood all our lives, but it was becoming impossible for us to stay there any longer. The fear and ignorance haunted us daily. Before AIDS, Alvinho was very popular and had many friends in the neighborhood, but when people started to find out that he had contracted AIDS, friends disappeared fast, even our closest relatives. Everybody was afraid. I was too, but he was my loving brother, and I would never abandon him. In fact, my sister told me one day, "If you fear for your life you don't have to come. I will understand." I told her that my place was with them in their hour of need. I couldn't live with myself if I had abandoned my family in this terrible time. I thought about my two daughters and my husband, but I put myself into God's hands, and went home again and again, as many times as it was necessary.

The second time that I went home to Brazil was because once more, Alvinho had called me home. The phone rang and when I answered I could feel the profound sadness in my brother's voice. For the first time, I could hear the sound of defeat coming from him. I wanted to scream but I couldn't. I wanted to say something, but no sound could come out of my mouth. I had to be strong for him, but at that moment, I, too, began to die a little. My question now was how I could help my little brother. How could I alleviate his sufferings, because I was already sharing in his suffering, but I wanted to make his life less miserable. I remember when I told him that I loved him and that I would go home right away, he started crying softly and said, thanks.

When my husband came home from work, he found me profoundly crying. My face was a mask of agony. I told him that my little brother had called again and that I needed to go and that I was already packing. Immediately I made arrangements to go home. At work I explained the situation to my manager, Smithy Dunn, a compassionate woman, and she let me take time off work. I bought my ticket and a few days later received my visa. I needed it because I had become an American citizen. A week later I was flying to Natal, but this time I was going home with a heavy heart.

When I arrived at the airport in Natal, for the first time in my life there was nobody waiting for me, so I took a taxi home. It felt as if death had already arrived at my house. What a difference from times before, when my family, my brothers and sister, and my friends welcomed me. I had always been received with joy and laughter. This time tears rolled down my face, I was afraid for my brother, for me and for my family. I had the feeling that everybody had already abandoned us. I prayed to the Lord asking for strength. I felt so limited, so miserable, incapable of bringing help to my brother. I couldn't bring him the cure that he so much wanted. When I arrived home Alvinho was the first one on the porch. I looked at him standing there, waiting for me with his arms stretched out; like a shipwrecked person trying to grab a piece of wood in the middle of the ocean. I knew that I couldn't bring him salvation. Lord, how hard did I pray to have strength. We embraced and cried. I knew that very soon he would start his ascent into Calvary. What a horrible feeling when one feels impotent, when one knows that the only thing one can do is suffer in silence. Being there for him was the only thing I could do. I wanted to absorb his pain, like I had wanted when he was a little boy with burnt feet. I wanted to bring him hope, but how could I bring hope and consolation for this intelligent young man when he knew that there was no hope? I could only imagine the depth of his despair.

I came into the house only to see more suffering, more desperation. My mother had a strong faith and was holding her own, although she was mortally wounded. But my sister Fatima was in despair and a few times I thought she was going to lose her mind. One day I saw my mother holding her and praying, as my sister was screaming again, "Alvinho, our Alvinho has AIDS, this is not happening, can't be happening to us."

Again, I had to try to help her and shake her. "I know this situation is horrible, but we must learn how to cope. Stop! You're not helping him acting like this." She stopped screaming and began crying softly, but it was as if someone had taken life out of her. She was leaning heavily on me and slowly was able to sit down, acting as if she was in a trance. I didn't know what else I could do. The situation was not very good at my house, and I was afraid that we would all end up losing our sanity.

I saw Alvinho coming from the back of the house, and without words, we hugged each other, holding tight to one another in an embrace of love, of true communion with Christ. We were there for each other; we were trying to support each other in our suffering. I never felt so close to my family then in that moment. Life is such a wonder; the unforgettable moments can be of profound joy or profound suffering. I knew I would never forget those moments of deep suffering. But like my grandma used to say, "The good time passes, but bad time passes also, everything passes in this life, so be strong for the journey." I was glad that my grandma was not alive to go through all this suffering but remembering her words helped me.

Some moments in our lives are truly unforgettable, another of these rare moments came when one day we were sitting at the kitchen table" Alvinho, Mom, my sister Fatima, and our nieces, Moema and Valeria and me. We never asked Alvinho embarrassing questions because we knew he was already embarrassed with the whole situation, but we were all there looking at each other trying to give him all the love and support that we could. Minutes later our brother, Bosco, came in, and also sat at the table. We told Alvinho how much we all loved him and that his sexual preference would not change our love for him. His sexual behavior was not important. He was important. He kept his head down as we talked, and we could feel his embarrassment. It was not easy for him knowing that his secret life was no secret anymore. With tears rolling down his face, he looked up at us and said nothing, but there was gratitude in his eyes. We understood him, and suddenly there was a feeling of peace among us that nobody could explain, there was silence, but it united us. That silence was worth a thousand words.

When we all left the table my brother Bosco, called me at the side, "Co, this is really church, this is really communion with God. I felt as if the Lord Jesus was there among us at the table." I told him.

"I know Bosco, the spirit of the Lord was probably among us because where is love, there is God."

Our love for Alvinho united us that day in holy communion. It was beautiful but it was also tragically sad. We all felt profound sadness, especially Alvinho. His face was a mask of sadness and shame, shame because our mother was among us and he knew how difficult it was for her to accept the behavior that had brought him his death sentence. We knew how terribly difficult it was for him. The only thing we could do was let him know that he was loved. We were not there to judge, but to give him our loving support.

Two weeks passed quickly, and I had to return home to my children, my husband, and my job. Leaving was also a difficult time, I felt more divided than ever because when I was in Brazil, I missed my children and husbands, and when in the United States, I missed my mother and siblings. My older brother Bosco took me to the airport, and only then at the airport could I have a good cry. I flew back to the States with my heart broken into thousands of pieces.

When I arrived at home in Tucson, I told Bill I wanted to buy a home for us in Brazil, a vacation home, but he knew my intention was to move my family from the neighborhood and go where people didn't know about my brother's condition. My husband gave me more than half of the money we had in our savings account. I couldn't believe his generosity when he said, "The money in the savings is our money, do you think that this will be enough?" I really didn't know if it would be sufficient. I prayed to the Sacred Heart of Jesus to help me find a home for the amount of money that I had. I asked St. Therese, the little flower, to pray with me to the Lord, and to give me a sign, and she gave it to me. One day I was in church after mass, I was finishing cleaning the dishes from this mass, when the sacristan came to me and said, "Please take some of these beautiful flower's home. We're going to throw them away and change the arrangements on the altar." I knew then that I was going to find a home to move my brother from the old neighborhood. It was our Catholic belief that if we received a flower at the time when we were praying St. Therese's novena, it was a sure sign that she would help us with our request.

When I was ready to go back to Brazil, I took all the money in cash. I stashed them under my clothes, my jacket was full of money, I had money inside my jeans, I had money down in my underclothes. I was scared to death to take the risk, but it was necessary and I believed the Lord was giving me His blessings. Bill was totally against the idea. He told me that this plan was insane because the cops in Brazil were going to find the money and we were going to lose it all and that I was going to end up in jail. Then he went out to the airport and got some forms for me to fill out and advised me to declare the money at the airport and forget about the crazy idea of carrying it with me. I told him I would do that, but I did not change my plans because I knew of a case where an American tourist had been killed by a police officer in Brazil for thirty thousand dollars. It was the amount of money that this man had declared before leaving the US. I wasn't going to trust the system there. I was carrying double that amount. I was so scared that I was numb with fear. I boarded the plane feeling as if I was carrying a bomb ready to explode at any moment. I was so nervous that I jumped at everything; my heart was racing, I had never prayed so hard in my life. Every minute was a prayer to the Almighty. After boarding the airplane, I didn't move from my seat but a few hours later I needed to go to the restroom. When I was inside the little bathroom a package with five thousand dollars fell from my waist into the airplane's toilet. I had to pull it out. Thank God, it was in a plastic bag. Then I had to put it in my purse. After that episode I was super careful not to drop anything, I was always touching and hugging my jacket. Finally, I landed in Natal, and once in the airport I told my brother Bosco what I had done. He agreed with me that I was safer doing what I had done. He thought I should have wired it through the banks. I knew that with cash in my hands I was going to make a better deal. People in Brazil wanted the dollar for travel and they would pay more on the black market.

Soon we started looking for a house to buy, but they were all too expensive. I knew we would find one, because it was for a worthy cause and the Lord was going to help us. After looking over many homes, my sister became discouraged and tired. I knew we would find our ideal house with the Lord's help. My brother Bosco remembered a friend who had had a house for sale the year before. We went to see his friend and the house was still for sale. I couldn't believe my eyes; it was perfect for us. It was worth more money than what I had brought, but the owner needed the American dollars to give to his wife who was going overseas on vacation. Bosco said to us, "You guys pray, pray that this guy accepts this amount in dollars, because if he accepts it, it will be a business from father to son." My sister said, like we say in Brazil, "E um negocio da China- it's a business from China." We all went down on our knees to thank God for the house. It was God's gift to us because after this man consulted with his son, who was a bank manager, he decided to accept our offer. We made the deal and got the new home. Thanks to God and my husband's generosity, we moved quickly to this new neighborhood. The day we moved, the people on our old street came outside looking at our belongings going into the truck in disbelief. We knew that we had to wait a few years before we could sell our old home. We followed the moving truck. It was tragic and comic at the same time. There was my brother Alvinho holding Louro, our parrot, who was talking and yelling, making an infernal noise, attracting the whole neighborhood's attention. Louro was probably very upset and scared, not knowing what was going on. We moved swiftly and quietly saying goodbye to no one, except to our lady neighbor across the street, Dilvinha Flor, who was a wonderful person. She had offered her beach house for us to move in if we wanted. We couldn't accept her generous offer.

To be able to move into our new house was wonderful, a true miracle, and we all felt as if we had won a big lottery prize. We all loved the house. Alvinho was very happy but unfortunately, he only lived there for a few months. Before we purchased the house, my mother said one intriguing thing to us. She asked us to please keep it quiet because the soul of a business is secrecy. Don't say a word to anyone, because we don't know what is in the hearts of men. Envy is worse than macumba, or voodoo. I never had heard her say such a thing, but we all followed her advice. This is the home that my sister and my mother still live in today. I believe this house It is another one of God's wonderful gifts to us. We couldn't believe the price, but it was just right because the Lord's hand was guiding us. I remembered Grandma saying to me, "He who trusts in the Lord will never be disappointed." I had put all my faith in the Lord and He didn't disappoint me. This house has a little garden with many flowers and tropical plants. Humming birds come every day, and many other birds sing in the mornings. It also came with a pair of beautiful chameleons; they live there free inside our small garden. The birds are also there delighting our ears and eyes with their songs and the beauty of their plumage.

It was a moment of grace when we came into this house. I know now that there is a reason for our sufferings, and it must be a good reason, because God's own son came down here and suffered terrible physical and emotional pain, and it was for a good reason. Only our creator knows why. He was humiliated like we were humiliated, and who were we? To ask for better treatment? However, I still don't understand the reason why we suffer. Maybe someday I will know. But Lord forgives me, it doesn't make any sense now when I only see and understand with my limited human eyes and mind. The only thing that I say is, "Jesus in you I trust. Father, Son, and Holy Spirit, I do trust you." And I do trust the Lord because I saw his mercy towards me, a sinner.

When I came back to Tucson I went to see a psychologist. I was feeling miserably confused. I didn't know what was right and what was wrong anymore. This professional educated me about homosexuality. The psychologist told me that people didn't have a choice, that some people were born gay, there was no choice. She mentioned the animal kingdom and explained that some animals are born gay, just like people and that perhaps it was a way for nature to use birth control. It was an eye-opener for me. I had never thought about it in this new way, and it gave me hope to talk with my family. I called home and started educating the rest of my family: my mother, my sister, my other brother, Bosco. I believe my mother understood, or I want to believe that she did, I hoped that with understanding she would suffer less. Because of her Catholic background, accepting that my brother was gay wasn't easy for her and yet she deeply loved her son. She couldn't reject him, nobody could. I know she was hurt and confused with her feelings as was everybody else in our family. But with our suffering we learn so much more about people, about life. We all hung on stoically for Alvinho. Never in my life had I seen a more profound expression of family love.

If someone asked my name, I would say my name is "sadness" because my mood never seemed to change. I would get up in the morning and say to myself, "Good morning sadness," and at night, "Good night sadness," and sadness became my daily companion. My mood was always the same, and my colorful world had turned gray. It happened so suddenly. I was living a nightmare. However, I was lucky. I had my American family to run to. Even before marrying, I told myself that if someday I had my own family, I would have a home where I would like to run to, not to run from. like I had done before. I would make my home my little nest, and I was successful doing it. My husband supported me at this terrible time, and I was grateful for that. I had made my little nest. I could come home and get busy with my chores. And in doing so I was doing some mental hygiene. I had my babies, my two daughters. It was not easy for my mom and my sister.

But my mother and my sister had only me, and I lived so far away in Tucson, Arizona. I was only able to visit them once a year because, besides the expensive airplane ticket, I had my job at the bank. Coming home to my two young daughters helped me because they needed me. I desperately needed them too. However, my heart and mind constantly went back to staying with my brother in Brazil. I never really left home; my heart was there too. Every morning, I took refuge in Jesus' heart. He was my strength, my fortress. It was good to get back to my routine, going to work and taking care of my husband and two daughters. I returned to Tucson mentally and physically exhausted.

Now with my family in Tucson, I could think more clearly. I called Natal daily to get a report about Alvinho's health from my sister and my mother. His health started to decline rapidly, and he was getting infection after infection; what the doctors called 'opportunistic infection'. The only known medicine to attack the AIDS virus was a drug called AZT, not yet available in Natal. It was too difficult to find a pharmacy in Sao Paulo or Rio de Janeiro that could send the medicine to my family. My sister asked if I could help get this medicine here in the States and send it to her. I started by asking my primary care doctor, and he said no, he couldn't do this for me. Then I went to see a specialist in infectious diseases, but the results were the same. He couldn't give me the prescription. Then I remembered a doctor that I had befriended a few years earlier when I was leader of a girls scouts group. This physician's daughter was in my group. I called that doctor and explained the situation. I was desperate. She agreed to give me two prescriptions which I immediately got filled. I ran to the airport and sent it to Brazil, but soon my brother needed more, and I knew that my friend's doctor wouldn't give me another prescription. I understood she could lose her medical license. When I came back, I gave her a beautiful stone that I had brought from Brazil. It wasn't a payment, but a thank you gesture. I could never pay her enough for her compassion. Giving my brother's medicine, she was putting her career at risk.

I was desperate once more and I couldn't take no for an answer. I decided to knock at another door. I went to TIHAN, an organization that supported AIDS patients here in Tucson. There I met a young man, Shawn, he was working at this organization.

He also had the AIDS virus. I told my story, and I couldn't hold back my tears because I had no other place to ask for help. This young man said to me, "Don't worry about it. Your brother will have the medicine he needs." I couldn't believe my ears. I felt such relief and hope again. Maybe my brother could be alive for few more months. Just the thought that I was helping him made me feel wonderful. Through his doctor, this young man supplied me with all the prescription medicine I needed until the day Alvinho passed away. After my brother's death we had some AZT left. Because this medicine was in great demand, my sister went back to the hospital and gave it to one of the doctors there. A year later my nieces came home to Natal and went to the hospital to visit the staff and donated some supplies, but I couldn't go back with them to the hospital. I just lack the nerve to see other people going through what we have gone through. Maybe someday I will go back. I know the need for everything remains, but I lack courage. It's something stronger than me. After almost twenty years, it's still too painful to think that such places exist. At the AIDS ward in Giselda Trigueiro, I met hell on earth, a place without hope. God help me that I may never need to be back there.

After my brother's death, I kept in touch with the young man here in Tucson, who helped us. Shawn became a dear friend and after my brother's passing, he, too, felt very ill and had to go to the hospital. My husband and I visited him at Kino hospital, and he wasn't doing well at all. Soon he passed away. I went to his mass at St. Augustine cathedral and saw his mother there. I was surprised because she wasn't in good health either. Indirectly she was another victim of AIDS, just like my mother whose health started to decline after my brother's death. The young man, Shawn, who helped me, was born in the United States, of Mexican descent, had many relatives and friends attending his service. They celebrated his passing with a beautiful mass. I was there with a heavy heart, remembering my brother's mass from which I had been absent. It was also painful to say good-bye to my friend; he was so young, handsome and so full of life. He had such a compassionate heart. He had helped my brother and me, two strangers to him, and I knew that God Almighty was not going to ask him to give account of his faults. He was going to see how much he had loved, and then He would say to him, "Well done my son, come with me and enter into your father's house." I believe there are many AIDS victims up there in God's city, because we all will be judged by love. Today I believe that being gay is not a choice, some people are born that way. It's not their fault, and God is just. Today my outlook toward the gay community has changed, and I respect and accept their way of life, as long as they respect and accept mine. We don't dance to the same music, but I have learned tolerance, respect and understanding towards the gay community because the person I loved most on this earth was gay.

This horrible illness called AIDS has taught me many lessons: one of them was humility, the other was awareness. There is a moment in our lives when God touches us with his grace, and we become enlightened. This happens without any work or effort on our part; it's all pure grace. This grace comes not because we deserve it but because God grants it to us; it is a divine mystery. Today I'm a humble person. I'm grateful for many things, but I understand that everything that I have isn't mine, it was all lent to me for a certain amount of time. When I leave this earth, I will go naked as when I was born, and only my soul will soar to the Lord's arms, this I do hope. By God's grace, I accepted my brother's cross and ours too.

Today I have joy in my heart, a joy that I thought I would never experience again. My three grandchildren are now the joy of my life, and life goes on with good and bad things happening to all of us. Like Vovo Titida said, "The good times come and go, but bad times come and go also, because everything in this life passes. The good times and the bad. One must be strong for the ride, because the future belongs to God alone."

A year after my brother's death, my friend Shawn became very ill, and when he moved back to his father's house, I visited him a few times. I found out that his mother was also ill with some serious respiratory problems, but his father was doing well. They were humble people, and I gave some gifts to them. Brought them baskets with food. It was just to let them know how grateful I was. I could never repay what Shawn had done for my brother and me. His father asked me one day, "Are you wealthy?" I said no, I'm a bank teller, but I share what God has given to me. The years passed by, and I wasn't remembering Shawn's family anymore, when one day my phone rang, and it was a man who identified himself as Shawn's father. He said to me, "I was hoping that I would find you. I want to tell you that I also learned how to share." He told me his wife had also passed away. It was nice to hear from Shaw's father but after that phone call I never heard from this man again. My gratitude to Shawn is forever in my heart. I believe the Lord has sent his people to help me throughout my life and it's only fair that I, too, help in any way I can. Shawn's father's phone call made me feel good, praise God. I had learned how to share with people in need at home with my family. My grandma and my mom always shared, my father also helped people in need. I remember my mother saying one day to my father, "You have many faults, but your charity is going to save you." I am sure my father wasn't happy to hear that. My Grandma, many times had said that poor was the devil, we Christians always had enough to share, if not material things, it would be a prayer, a hug and a kiss, a smile or a kind word, even when sometimes we were just listening to other people, this, too, could be an act of charity. Thanks to grandma, I know that I will never be poor, I will always have something to share with others, because poor is the devil, who can't feel love.

My mother is now 94 years old, and lives in the comfort of her home with my sister Fatima. My mom deserves what she has now; her life is good and peaceful. My father, who had held an important position in the government, left her with a good pension, and thanks be to God, my sister and my mother have no financial problems.

Now I go home twice a year. I know mom's life on this earth will soon stop, but it will not end. It will continue in another dimension. I can only imagine the happy reunion of my grandma Titida, my sister Eneida, my brother and my mom, and my father too. In God's time, I hope to be there also, enjoying the infinite love of this mystic God, sometimes an incomprehensive God, but nevertheless an awesome God, all-loving God. This God who loves is unconditional, and never denies help to his children, because of his own nature, His own essence, he can't deny help because He is love. When we ask with faith, He always gives. I believe He only denies what isn't good for us, and like a loving parent He never denies his help. Praise and glory be to God Almighty, who gives us strength, who makes us resilient in bad times, always renews our spirit and pours in it the joy of living, giving us a heart full of gladness after our tragedies and sufferings. Only a God could accomplish such a miracle of pouring into our spirit the grace of joy, and His peace. The peace that the world can't understand. I believe it was His peace and grace that made us survive after Alvinho's death, and make other people survive after the horrors of war, tsunami or any other tragedy. A thousand times I have asked my Lord, why? And I have no answer. I guess it isn't for me to know yet, only to have trust in Him, and as long as I have his grace, I will have faith. I will do just that. In Him I will trust.

    I remember, when we were young, talking among ourselves and when the subject happened to be death, my mother used to say, "I don't want to die young, death is an ugly, old rooster, without feathers, and when I see it, I will fight." She didn't die young, she is still living at ninety-four and a half, but what a long and painful journey her life was. I think that my mother used this simile, this silly comparison about death, because of my uncle Zuza, her brother, who used to raise roosters to fight, and after a fight, these poor old roosters without feathers, were revolting and the most pitiful thing to see. But like my mother said, unfortunately all of us will see some day this ugly and featherless old rooster.

Sometimes I feel that it is only by the grace of God that we keep the faith. In fact, I'm convinced of that, it's because of His love in our hearts that we find strength to continue our journey in faith. It's the hope to see Him face to face in the glory of our resurrection that keeps us going, it's a precious gift. My brother Bosco told me that he doesn't like to see Jesus hanging on the cross; he likes to see Him on the cross, but in glory. I like to see the image of Jesus in glory too, but we also need to see Him hanging on the cross because people need to be reminded all the time of His sacrifice.

It is the same with the victims of the holocaust. Young people today need to be reminded of the evil of Nazism; that horror should never be repeated in history. It's too frightful just to think about it. At a Jewish wedding I met an elderly lady, who told me she was a survivor of the holocaust. She was a young girl at the time and her whole family perished in a concentration camp. She was the only one who survived because she was liberated by the allied forces. She came to America and became a successful pharmacist, married a Jewish young man and had a boy and a girl. This lady seemed to be a happy person, thanks to the miracle of healing. She told me no human being deserves to suffer as her family did in the holocaust. I cried for her, and thought, Lord, why so much evil on this earth? Why did this happen to your people? I can imagine how many Jewish people asked the Lord the same question and this is precisely why I say we need the miracle of faith.

I remember how my brother was before being infected with the AIDS virus. He was so clean, so handsome, and so well dressed. He was a refined young man and had the manners of a diplomat. AIDS changed his physical appearance but not his inner self. AIDS also changed our family, not physically but internally. I believe nothing good can come from AIDS, but it was the vehicle that helped us to become better people. It was our suffering that changed us and led us to learn so much about homosexual behavior and showed our bias about the subject. Our rationality towards gays changed. We stopped looking at them as if they were a group of people apart from our society, apart from us. After the fatality of AIDS in our family we integrated them as one of us, because the person that we loved most in our lives was gay. I know it wasn't his choice. We started to look at the gay community for the first time as part of us. We started to understand, and with understanding, we began to accept the differences. We learned the hard way that blacks or whites, fat or skinny, old or young, straight or gay people were just like one of us, people living and suffering on this earth. There was no difference at all. No labels and no division were necessary because we were people, human beings with the same physical and psychological needs. But I had to go into therapy and learn that a homosexual had no choice, a person was born that way. It wasn't a question of choice like I used to think it was. I educated my family about the subject. I was surprised that my mother understood it very quickly, but it was not easy for her to accept the fact that her loving son was gay. She was afraid that God would condemn him, she was tormented by that rationale, but we told her that Alvinho's God was a God of love and mercy and that we believe in the same loving God. Nobody could judge, but only God could pass judgment, we were going to be judged by love. The Lord was going to look at Alvinho's heart and see how much he had loved here on earth, and only love was going to be important for his salvation; all the rest would be of less importance. I reminded her of the time when I had gone with Alvinho to the open market to buy food for the poor and take it to St. Anthony's church, where they later would distribute it among the destitute. I remember when I offered to pay for the food that he had purchased, he told me, "No Co, thanks, but I must pay with my own money. I promised it to St. Anthony. I told him." At that time, he was still a law school student with little money of his own. I reminded my mother of his loving and giving heart, of his humble and contrite heart. Our mother finally put her son into God's merciful hands, and I hope it gave her peace. Before my brother passed away, he understood the emptiness of parties, clothes, and other material things. He understood the unworthiness of public adulation. We all benefited from his discoveries; we all grew deeper in our spirituality and simplicity.

When our brother Alvinho was sick the only human behavior that still could surprise us, was an act of kindness from an acquaintance because we were used to the ugliness of human behavior. We learned to lean on each other and God. Together we stood tall because love is a very splendored thing and it united us with cords stronger than steel. One day one of our relatives bought a new car and came to our house to show it off. Alvinho asked to drive around with him in the new car but was refused because he had young children and it wasn't a good idea. My poor brother suffered one more humiliation and went inside the house in tears. He said, "I'm worse than a leper." We all hugged him, my sister, my mom, and our nieces, we all embraced him tightly, and I said to him, "Alvinho, we are all lepers, nobody is clean on this earth, my brother."

A few weeks later this same relative, who had the new car, needed my brother's service as an attorney because my brother would help him without charging him a fee. This person came to our home asking for his help in a very serious business situation. Already very weak, Alvinho changed his clothes and went with that person to his office and was able to help. I didn't say anything to my brother, but told my sister, "I now know the meaning of turning the other cheek, the meaning of forgiveness," This was Alvinho, always ready to help, always with a clean heart.

We knew a man who used to work for our cousin Bibi at her farm. He was Mr. Joao de Xixiu. Sometimes he delivered boxes with fruit to our home. He was an uneducated man but a philosopher in his own way; he used to say to our mother, "Godmother, humanity is a scoundrel." I don't believe that everybody is a scoundrel, but I'm tempted to agree that there are a great number of scoundrels on this earth and for this reason, I consider Mr. Xixiu, as one unforgettable man and a great philosopher. Nowadays, every time that somebody disappoints me, or treats me with unkindness, remembering Mr. Xixiu, I say to myself, "Humanity is nothing more than a scoundrel." He used to say in his peasant Portuguese, "Cumade, a manidade e canaia." It's much better to live with a clean and free heart, putting the trash in the garbage where it belongs and not inside us. It's too bad I only learned to act and think this way many years later in my life. What a wonderful University life is.

A week before my brother died, my mother had a dream. She called me to tell me about it, and I felt she was afraid. She told me that in her dream, she was lying down in her bed, and on top of her was a heavy cross. She was almost crushed by the weight of the cross, and she saw two handsome young men, dressed in white suits, coming closer to her. They removed the cross, but as soon as they removed it, she felt terrible. Immediately she missed her cross, because she loved it so much, so she yelled at them to please bring the cross back. But they quickly moved it away. I listened to her dream, and I understood. I was also afraid, but I said nothing about my feelings. I told her not to pay attention to the dream. But she insisted telling me, "But it was such a strange dream, such a vivid dream." A week later the angels took her beloved cross away: my brother went away from her forever. He passed away on a rainy morning, June 30, 1993.

We didn't know if the lack of money and resources were the government 's fault or if it was the administration fault. We befriended the director of the hospital, and he made our life a lot easier. We could stay with our brother at night, which was against regulations, but this director was a compassionate person, and also wonderful were all the other doctors who took care of our brother. Dr. Kleber and Dr. Eugenio went out of their way to help my brother. The nurses were also special people, but there was not enough money to run the hospital properly: no medicine, no cotton, no supplies, and no food for the other patients. Later on, I heard that the government controlled the hospital and there was no money from the government going into health care. Healthcare was not a priority on the politicians' agenda. However, ironically, the hospital had a few nutritionists on the staff, but no money to buy food for the patients.

We saw a tremendous amount of suffering among the AIDS patients. With my brother, there were six other AIDS patients. The man next door to my brother was a black man; he was skin and bones, looking like an old man and was already in the last stage of the disease. This man bit a nurse assistant when she was trying to brush his teeth. We saw the fear and desperation in this young nurse's eyes when she came out of his room telling the doctors what just had happened to her. A few days later this man passed away. The patient on the right side of my brother's room was a married man with two children, his young wife was being supportive, but who seemed to be hiding from everybody. She never stopped to say hello. Another patient, Jorge, was a well-educated young man from Peru, whose mother was a physician. He used to come and converse with us quite a lot. My brother enjoyed his company and we did too. Jorge told us that he had come and gone from the hospital a few times. Another was a young pretty girl, a prostitute who didn't look a day over sixteen. She was also skin and bones, but no one visited her, which made my heart ache. The other young man was a hairdresser. He was a happy fellow who seemed to be a bit of a philosopher. He told me that he had no one to blame but himself, and that his disease was a sign of the times. Death didn't seem to fright him yet. It was because he was healthy enough and the reality of an early death hadn't sunk in yet. He cut the hair of other patients at the hospital for free.

The last patient was the one who touched everyone's heart at the hospital, including patients and staff. He was an eight-year-old boy who was hemophilic. He had an angelic face and was a sweet little boy. His parents were very poor and couldn't afford to come and visit him because they lived in a small city in the interior and had other children at home. This boy only lived a few more months, but before he died, I saw a wonderful thing happen. Dr. Kleber, who was working with the AIDS patients, went beyond the line of duty and took this little boy to his home on weekends, letting him stay in his house playing with his children. This happened in 1992 when AIDS in Natal, Brazil, was considered worse than leprosy. To this day I've never forgotten this doctor because of his love and his compassionate heart. I found out through my sister that Dr. Kleber's two young boys are now doctors themselves. This doesn't surprise me because both of their parents were doctors. This was some of the more unforgettable loving human behavior that I witnessed at that hospital: a hospital that lacked everything but love between patients and staff. Soon I saw my brother's fear of being in the hospital disappear thanks to the caring and dedication of these people.

Alvinho was in the hospital for a few weeks and got better. The infection went away, and he came home looking very good. He gained weight and nobody would guess that he had AIDS because he looked very healthy. I came back home to the US with high expectations. I hoped a vaccine would be found or a cure could come, and my brother's life would be saved. I came home with hope that someone in the world would find a cure for AIDS. I thought my brother's life could be spared, perhaps Alvinho would find the strength to survive and find a way to live with the virus. I had high hopes.

We all had high hopes then a few weeks later he suddenly became ill with another infection. I was called home. Again, I flew to Natal. It was so hard for me to go, only because I knew that there was nothing I could do to help but just being there with them. I knew they all wanted my help and I couldn't help. This was very frustrating. I felt so impotent. I couldn't ease my brother's pain: he was carrying his cross to Calvary alone, and all I could do was watch. My pain also was enormous, but I knew that I only could imagine and comprehend part of his profound pain. Our stress was tremendous and there was nothing anyone could do to help us cope with the situation. We relied on ourselves for support. Dear Lord, at that time only You knew how heavy our cross was, it was crushing us, it had become too heavy.

When I was at home, one night I saw my mother trying to lift my brother from his bed. He was a tall man, and my mother was only four feet and eleven inches tall, but I saw her struggling. Together we sat him in his bed, but in the effort, I felt some warm liquid in my hands-his urine. We couldn't help him fast enough. The thought of being infected crossed my mind. I was still ignorant about this disease, and I thought about my daughters and became afraid of contracting this deadly disease. I prayed to God to protect me, because I wouldn't stop helping; I couldn't stop helping my family. I put my life and the lives of my sister and my nieces, Moema and Valeria, who had also left their home in Switzerland, into God's hand. My niece Moema at the time had a two-year-old little girl, Nahrla, who was there also. My nieces' presence helped Alvinho tremendously because they were like sisters to him. When my young sister Eneide passed away with Lupus at age 26, my mother raised the girls and Alvinho together, they were almost the same age. He became their uncle and their beloved brother also. My poor mother had felt the pain of losing her younger daughter in 1973, and now twenty years later, she was living the same pain all over again, only now it was worse because of the stigma of AIDS, the shame, the prejudice and the lack of community support.

    The day before Alvinho went back into the hospital for the last time I called him, it was in the morning here in Tucson, already early afternoon in Natal. We talked for a few minutes, and he told me that he was going back for some treatment because he wasn't feeling well. I told him that it was better for him to go, and he agreed with me. I remember his last words to me were "I love you, Co" which I answered, "I love you too, Alvinho." I could feel the sincerity in his words. He was saying it with all his heart, and I was saying it with all my love too, with all the love that I had for him in my heart. I didn't know then that it was our goodbye and the last time that I would talk to him, but now I think that he knew it was a goodbye. Three days later he was gone from our lives. Luckily my niece Valeria was in Natal, she had come from Switzerland, with her husband, and she told me to come home quickly, but I couldn't go fast enough because my visa expired. I bought my airplane ticket, but it was going to take a few days for the visa.

    Valeria called me the next day to tell me she was at Alvinho's bedside until the end, and she saw his passing. She told me that it was raining hard that day and she got up to close the window in Alvinho's hospital room, but he had asked her to keep the window open, he wanted to see the rain. Valeria said that few minutes later, after he had asked her to leave the window open to see the rain, a priest came into the room and offered him Holy Communion. He received our Lord in the sacrament, and my mother received it too. My mother was holding Alvinho's hand when, minutes later my niece's husband, who was in the room with her, saw him gasping for air, his eyes opened wide and in seconds, he was gone. My mother was still there holding his hand, not wanting to let it go when my sister, who had just left the room for a few minutes, came back and saw that he was gone from us. I was so thankful that my niece was there with Alvinho, my sister and my mother. She did for them what I would have done if I was there.

When I got home to Natal, my beloved brother was already buried. The situation at home was terrible. I found my mother and sister inconsolable. My mood certainly was not the best, but I had to pretend to be strong. I had to be strong for them and so I played the part. I wanted to go to his burial site that day, but I couldn't go to the cemetery. I was very tired from the long flight home and soon my mother became very ill. The next day, we called a physician friend of our family to our home, and he told us that he needed some blood tests from my mom. He also told us not to worry about her, she was fine, but we knew she wasn't fine. Our mother was not doing too well; I was afraid of losing her too. She was inconsolable in her grief. One day I saw how weak she was and holding her tightly I told her not to leave us, we needed her. Three weeks later she was doing better, and when the doctor came to see her, he told us she was fine now but she had life-threatening pneumonia. He didn't have the heart to let us know because we had just lost a brother. We thanked him for his charity, but we knew that our mother's life had been in danger. I believe that she fought for her life because of us, but she came close to following her beloved son.

Mom used to tell me that a mother's heart is like a fortune-teller, it knows the future. And I believe it, because many times we mothers do predict things, maybe because of the profound and intense love connection with our children. A mother's love is the closest to God's love on earth. If necessary, a mother gladly gives her own life to save her children, and nothing else can get closer to Jesus' love. My mother's dream was strange and amazing. It was a sign, and I know that she comprehended it. Deep in her heart she understood that she was going to lose my brother, her beloved cross.

I know in my heart that my brother found mercy with the Lord and is now looking over us. He is living in peace and happiness. I'm sure he is now immersed in the immeasurable ocean of mercy and love that is our Lord, and he is one in Him. He endured his heavy cross here on earth without complaints and now he is free. Where he is, nobody will ever close the door on his face because I'm sure that he was accepted in God's home. He is one with light, and he is light. I hope that someday we will meet again. I hope that by God's mercy, my brother will be allowed to meet me at the pearly gate. I'm not half as good as my grandma and brother. I can't fill their shoes, but by the grace of God, I hope someday I will join them where they are now. Alvinho finally went home to the city of God, the goal of all destinies. The day of his passing was a terrible day for us all. Our minds expected his passing; our intellect was accepting the inevitable. We knew as Christians that his eternal life had begun, but emotionally we were not ready, not yet. He had suffered physically, emotionally and spiritually, but we wanted him with us for a little longer. May the Lord forgive us for our selfishness, but we wanted him just a little longer among us.

Paradise for him here on earth was staying home listening to music, reading a good book, dancing samba at Carnaval in Salvador, going to parties, enjoying our green ocean and sunshine on weekends. Enjoying a glass of wine and a good dinner with friends. Now he has so much more that he can't miss these things at all. I'm sure that where he is now, he is at peace, experiencing true happiness. He has arrived home and now he understands it all, and his questions are answered. He is praising God, singing in the mornings the way he used to sing here on earth. Perhaps he says, "Lord, I'm finally a happy person because I'm one in You. I finally met the goal of my destiny. I'm home with You and now I understand." I know that when he was here among us, he was always pursuing happiness like the rest of us. I'm certain of this because one day when he was an adolescent, here in my home in Tucson, he asked me, "Co, why don't I feel completely happy here? I should be." and I said to him, "I don't know Alvinho, perhaps because you are missing home in Brazil." Now I know he is completely happy because finally he met God. True happiness can't be found on this earth, here we do have only moments of happiness, this is our reality and it's our faith that gives purpose to our lives.

College

After Alvinho's passage, I started to think how much he had insisted with me to go back to college, but I had never listened to him, I always had given few good reasons not to go, but now some force unknowing to me was pushing me forward to try. I told myself, I will try harder to accomplish my dream, it was a dialogue from earth to heavens, I told Alvinho, "my little brother, I will go back to college, I will do this for me and in your memory, you will see that I will graduate from college, I don't know how yet, but I will." I made this almost impossible promise to my brother from my heart.

I always wanted to have a profession. I wanted to become an attorney like many in my family before me. If that was not possible, I wanted to become a teacher. I remember my father telling me that teaching was a noble profession and that a teacher was like a needle opening the way for the thread to keep it going. However, he had opened the way for many ordinary people, but it didn't matter. The few good ones had given him great joy. My father loved to teach, and taught many people in our neighborhood, including our next-door neighbor, whose friendship he treasured. At night after dinner, these two friends would sit on the porch learning from each other. I remember Dad saying, when one teaches, one learns. It's not a one-way street, we are always learning. He said we learn in our neighborhood, at work, and on the streets, we are always learning. One stops learning only when one is dead.

Many times, my grandma said to me, "Co, when someone tells you something, you stop and think, and ask yourself this question, "Whom this will benefit? "This could be a matter of money, or any other issue, just ask yourself this question. Stop to think, don't jump to a conclusion. It's better to listen than to talk too much." Because of my grandma's teaching I learned to always ask this question: Who will benefit from this issue? And throughout my life, her teachings have helped me to make some right decisions.

After I got married, I told my husband that I would like to be an example for young immigrant children, show them that the American dream was still alive, and with hard work everything was possible. I told my husband that if I could go back to college and become a teacher, I would be giving back to America what it had given to me. I would try to inspire my students and show them their unique opportunity to live in the United States of America. Through a good education they could be accepted and become part of it. It was vital for them to feel accepted, not just admitted. I wanted to build a bridge between the immigrant community and the American community. I remembered the teachings of Paulo Freire, a Brazilian educator, whom I always admired, and I wanted to try to follow his teachings. I wanted to empower my students' parents and create that bridge between classrooms and community. I believed we all would benefit. I wanted to help my students think like they were part of this beautiful country. They had to learn to think as part of one great nation; we the American people; not us the Latinos, and them the Anglos. I would teach unity. My dream was to help my students to become good American citizens because the United States of America was a land of immigrants. They would learn to love it, but to love America, one needed to know and to understand its multicultural nature. I thought I could show them the way because I was an immigrant. I wanted to become a role model for my students.

My husband told me that college was out of question. It was too expensive and finally he asked, "Did you marry me to come to the US and go to college, or because you loved me?" I realized then how his insecurity was and that was the end of our conversation, but not the end of my dream. My husband's argument did not make sense to me, so I waited. My God would help me; I was sure of that. The time wasn't right yet, and I put the idea of going to college on hold. But when Alvinho passed away, I told myself the time is now for me to go back to college. My husband was still against the idea, but I was more sure than ever that I was ready to go back for a second chance. This time I had saved money for college.

We'd been married for many years, and Bill still did not support my idea of going back to college. I decided to go to Natal to try to arrange my university papers to be transferred to the University of Arizona. I did what was necessary, and the University of Rio Grande do Norte sent my official translated papers to the U of A. I applied to the College of Education, and I wrote my essay explaining to the College of Education why I wanted to become a teacher and how much I admired the tapestry of different cultures that made the spirit of the University of Arizona. Then I waited to see if I was accepted. I was so anxious. I knew my English was less than perfect, but I didn't ask for help when I wrote my essay. I had to enter the University on my own merit. If I could make it, so be it, and I tried my best.

The weeks passed and one day the mailman brought the envelope from the University. I looked at it and couldn't open it. I waited a few minutes to get courage. When I read it... yes, I was accepted! I was going to go to the College of Education! My God, my God! I couldn't believe how lucky I was. I praised the Lord. I yelled throughout the house, "God is great! God is great!" After that I cried with happiness, my heart ready to explode with so much joy, excitement and gratitude. Immediately I said, "Alvinho, little brother, I'm going to college; for me and for you. I'll finish the race, I promise you. I'm going to explore the last frontier." Yes! Now I really believe that in America everything is possible.

In the beginning of my life here in the United States, when I first told my husband about my desire to go back and finish my college degree, he sent me to a secretarial school in New Jersey. I was twenty-five. I went but only for the English classes. I had no intention of becoming a secretary. My desire to finish college was profound. I knew deep inside me that somehow someday I would have a college degree from this country. I knew that I had to find a way to go to college without my husband's financial help. In the meantime, inside me grew a deeper hunger for learning. It was a desire that wouldn't go away. I wanted to go to the University, and I wanted it badly. Many times, I thought of my father and how profoundly I had disappointed him when I decided to come to the US. without finishing my law degree. I had disappointed my mother and grandma when I married a divorced man in a civil law without God's blessings. I remembered many times grandma Titida saying that people who were married in men's law and not in God's law, weren't really being blessed. But when the time came to make my decision, I ignored Vovo Titida's teachings. Deep inside me I promised that someday with the Lord's help, I would make up to them. I didn't know how, but I would find a way. Few months later I found out that it was difficult for me to live without receiving the holy sacraments, and almost immediately I regretted leaving the Catholic Church. I wanted to go back to my mother's church but to do this, my husband had to ask for an annulment for his first marriage. I then started dreaming of the possibility of an annulment of my husband's first marriage.

However, a few years later, the Lord in His goodness granted me my two wishes. I was already married in law for eleven years and had my two daughters who were being prepared to receive first communion. A catholic priest in my parish, Msgr. Robert D. Fuller, Pastor at St Pius the X Catholic church in our neighborhood, helped us with the paperwork to obtain the annulment for my husband's first marriage. I am forever grateful to this priest. Without his help we couldn't obtain the annulment because my husband and I didn't know what to do to start the process. Because of God's grace and with the help from Msgr. Fuller, I was able to receive the annulment before my daughters' first communion. At their communion ceremony, I was able to join them in this celebration, and I received Our Lord's sacrament at mass for their first communion. At mass I cried the whole mass, and I don't know what the people thought. I was embarrassed but I couldn't stop. My tears were of joy and gratitude to God, my savior.

When I finally became a teacher, I went to work at Apollo Middle School, and I did exactly as I had planned. I taught my students the words of president J. F. Kennedy, "Don't ask what your country can do for you, but ask what you can do for your country." I was hoping that with the words of President Kennedy I could motivate patriotism among my students, because President Kennedy was a good communicator and a popular figure among the poor in many countries in South and Central America. My students knew about him before coming to class. I wanted to make the children of immigrants feel accepted. It was vital for them to learn this new culture in order to become productive Americans and good citizens.

I remember that in my essay I told the committee at the College of Education all my reasons why I wanted to become a teacher. I told them with a simple and sincere heart because I knew no fancy words.

After paying for the first semester, money was short. I decided to ask the University for a scholarship. I went to the department and the lady in charge told me that there was no money for scholarships and then showed me a pile of applicants who had applied before me. I told one of my teachers, Dr. Mary Carol Comb, that I had to leave college and I explained why. She advised me to talk with Dr. Luis Mall, another one of my teachers, and asked him about a scholarship. She was going to talk to him about that too. I went to Dr. Mall's office and told him my story that I already had asked for the scholarship and that it was denied. He smiled at me and said, "Yes, there is money, don't worry about it. You go back there tomorrow and talk with Carol, the secretary." Tell her I will send you.

Again, I went back to talk to the same lady who had given me a no for answer. I felt awkward and embarrassed, but as soon as I said hi, the secretary greeted me with smiles. She showed me a chair and brought a few papers for me to sign. It was the papers for a full scholarship, for the rest of my college education including a stipend for my books. I fought my tears. I didn't want the lady to see that I was crying. I couldn't believe my good fortune. With the scholarship my grades had to be an average of A or B. I couldn't afford to have a C average, or I would lose the scholarship. I knew I had hard work ahead, but I was delighted. I praised God for his goodness, because only the good Lord could have touched the heart of my teachers. I was still on cloud nine and couldn't believe my good fortune. Finally, I was going to become a teacher.

I remembered my father talking highly about the teaching profession, and how proud he was because he had taught someone. I, too, would become a teacher. I would be like a needle opening the way for others, I would be like a river, flowing with my mind, heart and soul. My spirit rejoiced. I would be able to touch the

American future through my students, and it was the realization of my American dream.

    I studied very hard because I knew I had to have good grades. I aimed for a B and most of the time got an A. Almost every teacher at the University was wonderful to me. I only met one teacher, who told me in her first class that her class was very hard, and I might not be able to pass. I needed her class to graduate, and I told her that I would stay in her class and try. I knew it was a big gamble. After hearing that teacher's comment my classmates literally pushed me to talk with the Vice Dean of the College of Education. Fortunately for me, she was a lady whom I had as a teacher in the semester before and I had passed her class with an average A. I really didn't want to make a complaint, but my peers didn't let me stay quiet. The vice-Dean told me not to worry about it and do my best. Next day I showed up to class, worried and scared but I stayed the whole semester. This teacher didn't know me. She just took one look at me and judged me as incompetent and stupid. It was a typical case of prejudice, but little she knew about me. I stayed around and passed her class with a B average.

    One semester before graduation my husband went to the hospital to have open-heart surgery. My stress was enormous. I told my adviser what was going on in my life, and my adviser told me that because of the circumstances, I would be allowed to finish college next semester. I thanked her and decided to try to finish my courses. I was studying for my finals and worrying about my husband's health. I was going from the University to the hospital where my husband was and then going home to study for my tests until late at night. Finally, he came out of the hospital, and I was able to graduate from college, but the stress had been too much. A week after my husband's open-heart surgery, I went into the hospital myself with a blood pressure issue. I knew it was caused by stress. Graduation day was a victory day, and I couldn't believe that I had earned a college degree. On graduation day I was walking as if in a dream.

After the ceremony I said to my husband, "Daddy, mission impossible accomplished. I'M A GRADUATED TEACHER. GLORY AND PRAISE TO GOD." Then in my heart I said to Alvinho, "Little brother, I have accomplished what I promised you. I'm a teacher, a college graduate from an American University." And at the graduation ceremony I cried, I couldn't hold my tears. I felt as if I was on top of the highest mountain. I was proud of myself, a great victory for me. I had achieved my dream, with God's help, my strong will, and hard work. I told my grandma, "Titida, your granddaughter is a teacher, and like you, I hope to become a good teacher. Like you, I hope not to forget to have fun with my students when I teach."

I remember that my grandma used to tell me that when she was teaching at the farm, she and her students had lots of fun and that they were learning together. She had made many field trips to the next farm with her class, and how wonderful it was to eat on the road, sitting under a mango tree, watching the kids run after butterflies. She told me that this was the way for her to bond with her students. My mother and my aunts always helped her with field trips. I never forgot her lesson, "First I bond with love, then I start teaching. The kids will learn more if they like you. Smile; it's fine to smile, they know you are the teacher but make them respect you. No student of mine was ever afraid of me, and yet they knew where I drew the line." I took her advice and the first day of school I was at the classroom door greeting my students with a smile. I know that I would make mistakes in my classroom, but I hope that the pluses weigh more than the minuses.

Even today I don't know how I had the strength to finish college; it was a marathon. It got harder at the end, but I finished the race. I asked myself how I did it, and who helped me; who gave me the stamina to try college for the second time? I know it was the Lord Jesus, my savior. I know it was my brother Alvinho who asked Jesus for me. It was my Grandma Titida also praying for me. It was my hard work and the help of many good people. It was a village helping me.

One day I received a miracle, and I believed it was Alvinho who helped me. When my husband was at the hospital recuperating from heart surgery, I had to take a hard test. I was not feeling well that day, but I had to go to the University and take that test. It was one of my finals before graduation. I was feeling overloaded. I was walking on campus towards my classroom, which was a good distance from where I had parked my car. I felt very weak and dizzy. I thought about Alvinho. I also prayed to Jesus to help me get to class and take the test.

Well, the most incredible thing happened. A young man came in a jeep, one of my classmates. I really didn't know him. He offered me a ride to class. I never had seen this young man in my class, never had paid attention to him, and now he offered me a ride. I got into the jeep and asked him, "Do you believe in angels?" He said, "Well I guess, why?" I told him I believed that he was an angel God sent to help me. I then told him that I was sick and how much I needed the ride. I knew without a shadow of doubt that the Lord Jesus or one of his angels was with me that day. It was a miracle, I can't explain.

I thought about my grandma and said to her, "Titida, our God is a faithful God, he helps us through generations after generations. He worked miracles in your life, and now He has shown his mercy towards me. Praise be His holy name."

After taking the test, I went to the hospital to see my husband and he was doing well. A few days later I took him home. Everything worked out well for me until the day of my graduation. Praise and glory be to God my helper.

My Daughter Moema's Lupus

When my daughter Moema was ten years old, she became sick and was diagnosed with Lupus. When I saw my little girl suffering from pain in her joints, I took her to the pediatrician. I had great fear because my younger sister Eneida, died at age 26 with Lupus and she had the same symptoms as my daughter was having. My daughter's pediatrician sent us to another doctor at the University Hospital, and there the doctor gave me the terrible news: my little baby girl also had lupus, the same illness that had killed my young sister.

With my daughter's diagnosis my fear took the proportion of a gigantic monster, and it crippled me. I knew then, profound suffering. I felt the terrific pain of not being able to do something to make her feel better and take her pain away. My little girl could not sleep because of the pain in her joints, and some nights I would fall asleep next to her bed, out of exhaustion. I was praying to God day and night, however I was angry at Him. My prayers were from my lips not from my heart. I couldn't look at her without crying, and sometimes I tried to avoid looking at her. Even if I didn't cry, just looking at her was sheer agony for me. I couldn't hide my suffering. My eyes showed pain, profound pain. I had always asked the Lord to let me hide my pain from others, to give me the strength to smile through my sufferings, because I always believed that when we smile to others we are charitable towards them, but this time it was impossible to do the charity of a smile, but I couldn't smile, I couldn't eat, and I was in profound misery. I didn't want to show my fears to my daughter, but she knew I was afraid

One day I decided to let the Lord know all my true feelings, as if He didn't know already. I told Him to take me instead of my daughter, that I love her so much. What kind of loving father was

He? He gave me a daughter and then he was going to take her away. At that point my eyes rested in a crucifix in front of me and I saw Jesus hanging in the cross for the first time. He was hanging there all the time, but I was blind. He was there in front of me, and yet I never saw Him. But suddenly something came over me, and I prayed with all my heart. For the first time I prayed with humility, love and acceptance. I said, "Lord, who am I to talk to you about love, about unconditional love? You gave your life for us, and I believe You suffered even more when you saw your mother's face on your way to Calvary, because in that moment in your human nature, You couldn't take her pain away, nor could You make your own pain disappear. You made the ultimate sacrifice to redeem us all. You are there hanging in this cross as a reminder of your sacrifice and love for us, but I, like a blind person and a fool, never really saw You. Forgive me Lord and do to my daughter whatever you want to do. She is yours, take her to You if it's your will. I am just her keeper for you, for a very short time. But Lord, stay with me, the pain is too much, and I will not survive without her if You don't give me Your strength."

After that prayer, I picked up the picture of Padre Pio off the table, and I started praying to him. I asked Padre Pio to pray for me to the Lord our God for my daughter's health. Padre Pio of Pietrelcina was a Capuchin monk from Italy, who had received the wounds of Christ and when he was alive, he healed many people. I began asking him to heal my daughter with the grace of God, and in faith I prayed with him daily. I asked the Lord night and day for my daughter's healing and Pe. Pio was asking the Lord for her cure too. I knew that he was a holy man and an elevated spirit on this earth, and the Lord would listen to him. He was a victim of love, he had become Christ on earth, he had embraced Jesus'cross, for love of God, and for humanity. "Pe. Pio, Pe. Pio, pray for us, pray for my daughter Mo and for me." It was my daily prayer to Pe. Pio. I begged him every minute of the day. A friend of mine gave me a relic from Pe. Pio: a very small piece of cloth with his blood, that had come from Italy, and I put it on my daughter. In a week's time I saw all my daughter's pain disappear. She slept during the night. She had no more symptoms of Lupus. I witnessed the miracle of God's power in my daughter's healing and through the mercy of Pe. Pio. The holy capuchin priest Pe. Pio, from San Giovanni Rotondo, a small city in Italy, a humble city but a city where God had chosen to have the most rich and brilliant diamond here on earth. Its rays were shining throughout the world, and many miracles and cures were received through Pe. Pio's prayers to God.

When I took my daughter back to the doctor, he told me her symptoms could come back later because there is no cure for Lupus. In my heart I said, "Never. It will never be back. What God heals, He heals. My daughter is free of Lupus forever." I lacked the courage to tell the doctor about the miracle because he was a man of science, perhaps a non-believer. But I was right, my daughter had been healed by Pe. Pio's prayers and by the grace of God. God and Pe. Pio had listened to the petitions of a mother's love.

A month later after my daughter's cure my husband, the girls and I went to Brazil. It was summertime there, and I knew that the sun was enemy number one of people suffering from lupus, but I was not afraid. My daughter went to the beach every day. She was under the strong tropic sun of the northeast of Brazil and never felt any pain. She was cured by the grace and love of God through the loving intercession of holy saint Padre Pio. Once more I thought about Vovo Titida, when she always said, "God doesn't give to people who deserve, he gives to people in need. He gives to those who believe and trust in Him."

My daughter is now in her forties, and she is doing wonderfully. She never felt sick or had pain again, and she has remained completely healthy—climbing mountains, loving the outdoors, and living life with strength and joy. Today she is also a successful restaurant owner, and I thank God and Pe. Pio for this miracle.

In the summer of 2000, my daughter and my husband and I went to San Giovanni Rotondo, the place where Pe, Pio had lived in Italy, to honor, to thank and to pray in thanksgiving for Moema's cure. When we went to rent a car in Rome, the people at the rental car company advised us not to go to San Giovanni Rotondo. They said that the south of Italy was dangerous, and San Giovanni Rotondo, was very dangerous. My husband was afraid, and my daughter told me, mom maybe it's better for us to stay here in Rome. I said no, we came this far, we are going to thank Pe. Pio for his prayers to God for your health. We will go do this at San Giovanni Rotondo. We had to pay more for car insurance, but we rented the car and went south.

Coming back from the rental car place, I saw a church close to our hotel. I went inside the Church of the Sacred Heart of Jesus. There I saw a picture of Pe. Pio and told myself Pe. Pio is going to guide us to San Giovanni Rotondo, and I believe he did. The trip was wonderful, the hotel was good and the food was the best. Not even in Rome had we had such good Italian food and the people in town were wonderful.

At San Giovanni Rotondo, we stayed in a hotel far from the church and the city. Our hotel was up a hill with a full view of the friary and the church. The view was beautiful at night. From the window in my room, I could see the place where a saint, a holy man, had lived, received the stigmata, suffered and died for love of God and mankind. It was very peaceful at San Giovanni Rotondo, and it felt as if the whole town was holy ground. We visited the church, Pe. Pio's room, and his tomb. In church we prayed giving thanks for the miracle that we received from the Lord through his intercession. We saw Pe. Pio's clothes, some with marks of his holy blood, the blood of Christ, the blood he had accepted to shed for the love of God and God's people. His holy cross was also heavy, but he carried it until the end, for the good of all. He became another Christ on earth. All praise be to God, because in my profound pain and agony He heard my cry. This was my big miracle. I have no medical explanation for what happened to my daughter. I can only explain her cure by the power and grace of God. Still today, I know of no cure for Lupus. My daughter is forever free from this disease.

When my grandma was alive, she told me many little miracles that had happened in her life. I listened and believed her. Now I see them happening in my life too: they are big and small. It's with humility that I describe them here, hoping that someday my grandchildren will read these words and believe, as I believed my Grandma Titida, when she told me about miracles in her life.

When Saint Francis Assisi said that is in giving that we receive, I thought it was all about spiritual receiving, and yet I witnessed a little miracle in my life, and it was about a material gift that I sent to my mother. One day when my girls were young, perhaps six and seven years old, I was talking to my mother over the phone. I told her that I had a beautiful Nativity set and she told me that her Nativity Set was too old, and that she would love to have a new one, but it was hard to find a pretty one in Natal. Our conversation was around the month of September, and after talking to her, I figured out that if I sent her my nativity set right the way, she would have it for Christmas. A week later I called her again and told her that my Nativity set was in the mail and it should arrive in December before Christmas. She was excited and loved the idea. I told her that I had the money saved to buy another set for myself. I waited for the month of December to come and went looking for another nativity set. I had saved one hundred dollars, and I thought it would be enough as my old nativity set had cost only sixty dollars. I went to some popular stores looking for a nativity set, but I couldn't find one I liked. Then I went to a more expensive store, and I found a beautiful nativity set, but it was three times more expensive; three hundred dollars. My heart sank. I couldn't afford it. I went home feeling defeated. I was sad, and I told the Lord, "Well, Lord this year will be the first year that I will not have Your infant image in my home at Christmas, but it's fine, I'm happy for my mother, this year she has her beautiful nativity set. I will save more and next year, I will have a nativity set in my home."

My husband knew of my disappointment and said nothing, but the next day he called and asked me to go to the hospital where he worked, to look at something. When I got there it was a Nativity Set that the nuns were raffling. It was a beautiful set. My husband told me that he had bought a raffle ticket. I became angry with him. I said, how naive you are, do you think that I have a chance to win? I bet these nuns already bought hundreds of tickets. Then he told me to look at the nativity set again, how beautiful it was, but I didn't want to look at it again. I left the hospital telling myself that it was gorgeous, but some lucky nun was going to get it, not me.

December twenty third arrived very fast. I was preparing my home for Christmas. I glanced at the place where I used to put the nativity set and resigned myself to wait for another one, next year. Three o'clock on Christmas Eve my doorbell rang. I opened the door and standing in front of me was my husband's coworker, John, holding two great big boxes. "Congratulations you won the Nativity set." I couldn't believe my ears, I said, "What?" and John repeated, "You won the nativity set, the raffle from St. Joseph's Hospital." I felt the tears come to my eyes. I tried to swallow them because I was embarrassed to cry in front of John. I WON THE NATIVITY SET. I couldn't believe my good fortune. Or was it a gift from the baby Jesus above? I choose to believe it was a gift from Jesus the Son of God. I called it my Christmas miracle, and like Saint Francis said, it is in giving that we receive. With love, I gave my nativity set to my mom. Jesus gave another nativity set from His heart to me. Bless the Lord, for His mercy is forever.

****

Today, eighteen years after Alvinho's death, I took the chance of telling my brother's story and mine. Mine is just the journey of a Brazilian immigrant, a young lady trying to figure out all about life. Finally, I got the nerve to begin undressing my soul in front of my children and grandchildren. I want them to understand a little more about me because sometimes it feels as if I have a brick wall between my daughters and me. I blame myself for the lack of communication and understanding. I blame it on the cultural shock too. Many times, I felt stupid because I couldn't understand American culture, and I should. Although I tried my best to acquire it, for me it wasn't enough what I have learned. I find myself laughing thinking, dear Lord I need another forty years here to learn the soul of the American people.

Lucky for me, when my daughters were little, I had a good neighbor who was a teacher. I asked for her help. She had two little boys, who were my daughters' age. I asked her to teach me all the little Mother Goose rhymes. I took my daughters to the library; I took them to piano lessons, ballet lessons and self-defense classes. We even went caroling through the neighborhood at Christmas time with my friend and neighbor Candy and her boys. I became a Girls Scout leader. I did all that I could to be involved in the American way of life. I tried my hardest to be the best mother for my daughters.

One day one of my daughters, who was about twelve and entering her adolescent years, told me, "Mom, I wish you were an American mother."

I felt like I had a knife cutting through me, but I said to her, "Sweetheart, I wish I could be an American mother too. I wish I wouldn't have this heavy accent when I speak. I wouldn't embarrass you, but do you know what? No American mother could love you more than I do." I know she was immature, and she didn't know how much she hurt me, but I wished I could have done better and could make her proud of me.

That day I cried silently. Even though I understood that she was just being difficult because of her age, I thought, if I had stayed in Brazil, finished my law school and married a Brazilian man, my daughters would be proud of me and not embarrassed. I just made a mess of my life. I couldn't even speak English well after all these years living here in America. My daughters were growing up without cousins, uncles, aunts or grandmothers. They didn't have the support that I had. I felt sorry for them, and I remember the saying, 'it takes a village to raise a child,' and I believe it does.

Today I feel that this is the right time to let my children know about my journey in America, about my journey on this earth, and how hard it was for me to assimilate another culture. I want them to know about my struggles and my determination to become part of this society and to feel accepted. But despite every heartache, every mountain that I had to climb, and every emotional pain that I went through, today I feel that I'm a winner. It was all worthwhile because of my daughters. They made my life sweet. They gave purpose to my life.

I have raised two beautiful and compassionate young ladies, who are wonderful mothers. They make me the happiest grandmother on earth. I want them to know how proud I am of them. They became the people that I dreamt they would be. Together we went through thick and thin, and I know I failed them sometimes; not because I wasn't born in the United States, but because I'm a human being. Like anybody else, I learned through trials and errors. I became an American citizen by choice, and now I will defend this country with my own blood if necessary. It is the country I love, it is my home sweet home, the land of the brave and of the free.

My son-in-law, Lucas Daniels, is serving in the Air Force. He went to Afghanistan seven times. I believe he served his country well and I know that if necessary, he will fight again and again for his country. We all will give our blood and will fight for our freedom, if necessary, because without freedom, life isn't worth living.

Finally, I feel that I belong here. I have roots in this good land and I feel accepted. I became a teacher, and I used my intellect, but also taught with my heart and soul for a few good years like I always wanted. I taught the sons and daughters of immigrants. I shared with them my experiences; I showed them that everything is still possible in America. One needs only to try hard and fight to achieve their American dream. But it is also necessary to have faith and to believe, to keep one's dream alive, because there is magic in believing.

I believe that all through my life, the Lord has been my shepherd. His light has brightened my path. He was my strength and my helper. I never carried my cross alone, in my sorrows and in my joys, the Lord was always nearby. My story isn't an extraordinary story, but I hope it will be important for my grandchildren, because it is my story and theirs too. It's a true story of a Brazilian immigrant, fighting for her dreams and coming out victoriously. And because I'm their Vovo I want them to be proud of me too. My story is the trajectory of my soul down here on earth because the body isn't that important. What is really important is invisible to our eyes. Everything else is an illusion: money, power, and possessions, our own bodies are so limited, only the spirit is real. We were created from an immortal God, we were created in His image, from the greatness of this God, and nothing down here is going to fulfill our souls. Some day we will soar like the eagle and then we will understand the pains and joys of this earthly life, but until then, only by the grace of faith will we be able to say, "Yes Lord, you will be done on me a sinner."

I know that my soul is like a drop of rain coming from the heavens. It has to come down and moisturize the earth and make it become fertile. We all can do this by loving one another. We are God's children, for some reason sent down here to learn how to love. But as soon as we get here, we are already looking up, getting ready to become strong to go back because we never really did belong down here. Like Grandma Titida used to say, "As all waters go back to the ocean, all souls go back to God." I'm seeing the winter of my life approaching, and I thank God for all His favors to me. I thank Him for my family, for the sun setting and the sun rising, and for the song of the bird on the spring morning, bringing so much joy into my life. My spirit rejoices in Jesus my savior, Deo Gratias. Today I'm a little like my grandma. I belong to a prayer group in my church, and I pray for my needs and the needs of others because I do believe that prayers work more than this world dreams of. Vovo Titida was a woman of faith, action and prayers. I'm proud to be a little like her. My strength comes from my faith, a gift from above.

I went to mass to celebrate St. Patrick's Day. Father Harry is Irish, and we had a good time after mass drinking Mimosas and talking. Little did I expect a call from my sister.

A daughter's goodbye

Tonight, March 17, 2010, Saint Patrick's Day, at 10 p.m. Brazil time, six p.m. Tucson time, my mother passed away. She was ninety-four and a half years old. I cried when I heard the sad news from my sister Fatima. It was an uncontrollable cry. I felt a terrible pain ripping through my not so young heart. My sister called me only a few hours after my mother's death, and my heart physically aches when I hear the news. Unfortunately, I can't go home to pay respects to my mother. Lord, it hurts. It hurts not to be able to say my last goodbye to her. But we have our plans, and the Lord has His. All my life I have asked Him to let me be there for her at her last hour, but with a broken hand in a cast, it was impossible to travel so far. There must be a reason for me to have this broken right hand. However, the Lord has given my mother another daughter to be close to her and to my sister. She is Zelia, a dear sister in Christ. She was there in my place, and she did much more than I could. As a physician, she has given her time and expertise to my mom and to my sister- 24/7. Dra. Zelia Fernandes took care of my sister, who was devastated, and at my mom's funeral. She made all arrangements for the burial. She told me my mom had passed away at the hospital, and mom passed away peacefully. Our friend Zelia, was mom and my sister's guardian angel, sent by the Lord to help my mom and my sister in this difficult hour. She did for them what I would do if I could have been there.

I was told that Mom was given oxygen and at the end she. She had peacefully passed away. Close to the end, my mom threw a kiss to my sister, and this made me realize that she was conscious until her last breath. My sister Fatima told me that near the end Mom also opened her eyes and looked surprised. Then she smiled the most beautiful smile, as if she was surprised to see someone she knew in front of her. I want to believe that she saw some spirit, who was there to guide her home; perhaps my grandma, my sister Eneida or my brother Alvinho. Or maybe it was an angel of the Lord ready to take her home. I would like to think that Padre Pio of Pietercina, or the Lord Jesus, himself, was there to guide her home. My mother's physical and emotional suffering were profound, yet she never complained about her pains.

When I left home to come to the US, I made my mother cry bitter tears, and only now can I understand and imagine how much she suffered for me. Only after I had become a mother could I fully understand her suffering. Mom never approved my decision to immigrate to the United States, and she always suffered because I was living so far from home. Only now do I understand her feelings because I wouldn't like one of my daughters to live in another city, much less leave home and live on another continent. I also suffered because I missed her so much too. If she only knew how much. She was right; I should never leave family, culture and country. I never told Mom how much I missed her and how hard it was for me to be away from the family. Somehow, I know that she knew in her heart that it wasn't easy for me either.

My dear mom, my sweet, sweet mother is now in heaven, next to my brother Alvinho, my sister Eneida, and our beloved grandma, Vovo Titida. Of course, I hope my father will be there too, transformed by God's love, which I believe is also possible.

But now my soul is dressing black. I am profoundly sad, my mom died and part of me also died with her but part of her will be always living with me. Oh! Dear God, today I need Your grace more than ever. I need your strength. I need your love. I am like a little child running to You, resting my head in Your lap, saying Lord, you are now my father and my mother, "Lord I believe, help my unbelief." In Your mercy, make my faith a strong faith, take my sadness and my pain and use it for the good of all your children. I put it at the foot of Your holy cross. I don't understand our human suffering, but Jesus I trust in you. Amen." MOM, I will LOVE YOU ALWAYS.

Goodbye Mom. Thank you for loving me, thank you for giving me life, thank you, thank you, thank you, thank you. Rest now in Jesus arms, rest in peace, dear mom. You, like nobody else, deserve eternal rest. Mom, I must confess to you the great silence scares me. I hope when you go through the valley of shadows, the Lord will shine His light to illuminate your way because you were his faithful servant. Lord make her brave, give her your strength, shine your light on her way, guide her through her path.

"Mommy, presence that is now absent," saudade, cutting through my soul. (Saudade, Portuguese word when someone is homesick, when someone is terribly missing someone.) Today I cry in silence, my being is saturated with saudades… because today I lost my Mom and my true friend, the person who knew me with my faults and virtues, and yet she loved me the way I was, she loved me whole.

Today ends the circle of my mother's life, a life of love, suffering and dedication to her family. Today I already see the sunset of my life approaching but I believe as a Christian, it's at the end of human life that eternal life begins. We are visitors to this planet. When the time comes for me to leave, I will miss my daughters and grandchildren, but I know that I will be reunited with my loved ones who will be there waiting for me to take me to our eternal home. Help me God that my spirit will never come back to see this earth again. Passing through this valley of tears; one time is enough. I hope that in His compassion, the Lord will take me home. Not because I deserve it, but because I'm His child and down here on earth I tried to love the best I could. I made many mistakes, but I always tried to do my best to repair some of the damage. It was never my intention to hurt anyone.

Thank you, Lord, for 94 and a half years of mother's life. You will understand my sadness Lord, the treasure that once was mine I lost because you have called her home. You took her back, and now I'm poor but you let me have her for a long time. I understand and I'm thankful. Please, guard her for me, keep her safe, and give her back to me some day when You will call me home. At that time let me hear her happy laugh, her jokes, her singing. But for now, keep her safely with You in the vast ocean of your infinity mercy. I know you are a mystery, and we are also mystics like you, please help me to be patient, and not try to understand the magnitude of Your plans. Because of your son's loving sacrifice for us, in confidence I say, JESUS SON OF THE LIVING GOD, I TRUST IN YOU. Thank you for my wonderful mother. "Mae, this is my goodbye to you, rest in peace, you deserve it. May the light of the Lord forever be surrounding you."

Your loving daughter, who will miss you forever. Saudades. Co.

It's only by the grace of God that I made it up to now into the winter of my existence and I'm continuingly saying, "Lord I believe and trust in You. I give thanks to You for the feeling of peace. I know it's God's peace, this peace that has no explanation to the world. Nevertheless, it exists. It's real because love exists, and this is why I believe. God, the supreme power, is also the supreme lover.

March 17, 2010.

With the passing of my mother, my brother Bosco told me that I had the right to ask for my mother's will. My mother had made my sister Fatima her curator, she did take care of my mother until mother's death. He told me that a great amount of money was in the bank, in my sister's name. My sister had never been married, nor had worked in her life, but she took care of my mom, and she saved and invested mom's money wisely all these years. My brother thought it would be fair to have the money divided among us, but my sister told me the money was hers because my mother had given it to her. I asked for the paper signed by my mother making this donation and my sister told me there was no paper; it was my mother's wish. I remember that one time my mother had said to me that all she had at the bank was my sister, because my sister wasn't married. I believed my sister; our mother was always concerned about my sister's future. She wanted financial security for her. I stopped to think, and I asked the Lord for His help, "What shall I do

Lord?" What is the right thing to do? My sister was getting a good pension from my mom, the same pension that was from my father, and it was now going to her by law. She didn't need all the money; however, I thought, she doesn't have a family, she doesn't have a husband, or a companion. She saved this money, my mother gave it to her verbally, and she is alone today. All that she has now is this money and it gives her security, because I live in the United States and also my two nieces live in Switzerland. My sister has nobody near her. I couldn't agree with my brother who asked for the money to be divided. The money was my sisters, and nobody should fight for It. It was Mother's wishes. However, until today I felt guilty, like Pilates, I washed my hands. I believe if I had said no to my brother, he would have listened to me. For This reason, they are enemies until today.

My brother Bosco wanted the money to be divided among us equally, but he understood my rationale and supported my decision. However, he said that he was going to fight in court for the money because it was mother's money. At that time, I told him, do what you think is right. Then I felt like a traitor. Today I think that I should say. No, don't do that.

I'm praying for my sister and my brother that they find peace among themselves and some day we will become a close family again. Like the psalm says, "Behold, how good is, and how pleasant, where brethren dwell as one!" I hope to live to see the day when we will be together again around the kitchen table in loving communion. I believe this could be possible someday, perhaps in a better place because what seems impossible for us isn't impossible for the Lord to do. I hope someday He will heal our hearts, and forgiveness and peace will prevail. Grandma Tilda always said that blood was thicker than water and peace among family was most important. I will never forget the day when we were together supporting Alvinho, sitting around the kitchen table, in total communion with love and with God. Our pain was profound but also profound was our love for our young brother. I remember the bad times, but I also remember the good times.

Life is wonderful, what a journey! I believe I was well loved by grandma, who loved intensely. Now my grandchildren are my true love ones. I melt in tenderness looking at their innocent eyes. Today for me there are not too many goals to achieve, or too many dreams to be dreamed. But I still feel the creative force inside me, and as long as I live, as long as I am breathing in this old body, I will continue to love life and to dream my dreams, because as grandma always said, "The heart never wrinkles." I will enjoy life until my last breath, and I will exit this world with a song of thanksgiving in my heart, praising the Lord our God for all the beauty of the earth and its goodness and for all the love found in the human heart, because only love makes the difference. As for my disappointments, my pain, and hurts, my disbelief; I will make a bundle of them and will put it at the foot of the cross. I will offer all to my beloved Jesus, as a gift, together with His sufferings, to give them to the Father. However, I will go from this earth without understanding the reason for our human suffering. Out of love and in confidence I will say like my Lord Jesus said, "Thy will be done" because all through my life the Lord has provided for me and for my family and in Him, I always will trust.

And here ends my little story, not an insignificant story, because this is a story of a soul, and all souls are important in God's eyes. This is the story of a simple woman, an immigrant from Brazil, who came, worked, and fought for her dreams. Like Cesar, I also say, "I came, I saw, I conquered." I conquered my little space in life, I earned a degree from a U.S. University, I became a teacher, a mother and a grandmother of three beautiful, wonderful children. I'm also so very proud that I am an American. I am also proud of my jobs as a bank teller and as a teacher. I taught the children of

Mexican immigrants for a few good years. My goal was to mold them into good American citizens and build the bridge between 'us' immigrants and 'them', the Americans. I wanted to show my students that the way to belong, to feel accepted in America, was through education.

My goal was also to be able to help the children with their dreams and transform this gap "them and us," into us the American people. A proud nation made of people of many lands. I agree with the Brazilian educator Paulo Freire who said education is political. I agreed with his rationale that it is our duty to become politically involved within our communities, especially now when immigration is such a hot topic. I also repeat what my father used to say, education is the Holy Grail, it may be difficult to get but it's worth it to try and to run for it. I believed when I was teaching these immigrant children, I was touching, helping and molding the future of this great country.

But it's with a heavy heart that I hear and see now on TV the politicians in Arizona fighting to create a wall between these two countries, Mexico and the US. Why doesn't the government create another '' Braceros '' program, similar to the one they had at the time of World War II? Why not try to create a better one, learning from the mistakes of the old program? Both governments-Mexican and American- could try to help the people who want to come here and work for a better life. It was done before at the time of World War II, it's part of Arizona's history, and it worked. The program wasn't perfect, but it helped. Why do Mexican and American governments don't try a good solution for these problems instead of building a wall to separate the two countries? Let's keep the drug dealers out of this country, but let the honest people who want to work come and work here. I believe they need jobs here, but we also need them. Some people can't afford to pay for an American company to clean their homes, but they can afford to pay a lot less to an undocumented lady to do the same job, and in the process, we are helping each other. This type of trade will not break the country. I understand that the United States has great economic problems now, but let's not blame it all on the immigrants. It's ridiculous and unfair. Now when I read Emma Lazarous' poem, I read it with mixed feelings and tears rolled down my face. I still have faith in America and believe the people in the US are good people, but it is our representatives, our politicians who are disappointing us. Where are the good old American values? Is economics taking over the consciences of our elected representatives? But where else can one find a Democratic system so close to democratic ideals, if not in America? Here we are still respecting the Constitution, the law of the land, and we can see Muslim mosques going up in many American towns, hand in hand with our Christian churches. All this in the name of freedom. Dear Lord, I'm proud to be an American. When Paulo Freire said that education was political, he also saying that nobody should stay in the middle, we have the right to choose because when we become educated, we all become political. We acquire a political view and a political voice, and it's our duty to express our views among our communities. Sometimes in a democratic way, one's pen becomes a battleground, a trench from which one can advocate his or her political views because of our freedom of the press.

I want you Rohwan, Asher and Riley to know that your Vovo always had a political opinion and fought for the underdog. We can't separate freedom from America because America is freedom, and we need to remind our children of the privilege and right to use this freedom. It costs the blood of our people, the blood of young Americans. It is still being spilled today in the name of freedom and for this reason our freedom is priceless. Never take it for granted.

Unfortunately, today there is fear taking over the country, and I often wonder if xenophobia isn't contagious. I want to keep my vision of this problem in a positive note; however, this immigration problem is very complex, and almost all of us immigrants at one time or another suffered prejudice. First were the Jews, the Catholics, the Irish, the Negroes, the women and so on. This isn't a new problem. However, it's remarkable that now we have a Negro as President of the United States of America. What an extraordinary victory over prejudice, what a success story, only in America could this be possible.

    I witnessed another great act of Americans when we all came together after three thousand people died in New York in the terrorist act of September 11, 2011; innocent people victims of an act of Islamic terrorists. Now I see this place become holy ground. It is holy ground for all mankind because it's not a place where only Christians died, but people of all faiths. For this reason, the only church allowed there should be an ecumenical church, a church of all faiths. This way we will be representing and honoring everybody, all the people of different faiths who died there. Let's never forget that three thousand innocent people have died in New York because of one act of Muslim terrorists and remember that this was not an act representing all Muslim people. I believe that not every Muslim is a terrorist. Americans are compassionate people. We aren't people who go to extremes to keep the illegal immigrant from coming by using force because it would be totally anti-American. I have confidence that the American government will find a solution for this problem. May God help us all who are now living in the US and love this country: the powerful ones, the rich, the politicians and the not so powerful ones. May God bless us, the ordinary people of America, because we are all brothers and sisters and we are all important in God's eyes. We, too, make a difference in this world. We are the American people and together, in unity, we can do a lot more than we think. This wonderful country is still the leader of the world. We have big social and economic problems, but for every problem there will be a solution.

We have come a long way, and we are resilient people; we will find a way to solve it all because in God we trust. This is the American way as long as we take refuge under the protection of the Almighty I will not fear for this country, now my country by choice.

Today September 15, 2011, started as it did two years ago, when I was looking at the Catalina mountains enjoying the rain, and at the same time being inspired to write my memories. They poured into my mind just like the rain. Now the monsoon is blessing us again, bringing heavy rain. The mountains are giving us a grand spectacle. Lightning and thunder fill the sky over the mountains, covering them with dark clouds. Today I can see nature repeating itself, and only by coincidence have I ended my writings on this rainy day. I like it this way. I want to think that nature is giving me a round of applause and is saying, "Well done. You finally did it; you wrote parts of your story. It may never become a best seller, but it's your story. It's unique; it has your mark on it. It is the story of your soul's trajectory on this earth. "I'm smiling, because it isn't important if I wrote it well or not. What is important is that I wrote it for my grandchildren. I wrote with emotion, mind and spirit.

In January of this year, I had to put a pacemaker in my heart and a doctor from Pima Heart Hospital here in Tucson put it in wrong. I had to have a second surgery to fix the mistake and Dr. Julia Indik from the University of Arizona corrected it. The need for the second surgery was an unpleasant surprise because I never expected it, but doctors make mistakes, and bad ones sometimes. However, tomorrow my husband and I will fly back to Italy, and God willing, I will enjoy every moment of this trip. I'm going back to San Giovanni Rotondo to give thanks to my God, our Lord Jesus Christ and to Pe. Pio my forever friend in heaven. There I will walk on holy ground, and with a contrite heart I will sing God's praise.

Epilogue

Finally in America, I became myself, I met my destiny and now I give praise to God, the One who guided me here. I'm sure it was His grace that brought me this far, and now I will wait until the day when I finally meet Him face to face, my Lord, my God, the goal of all destinies.

In my life many of my dreams come true. I came to live in the United States of America and became a teacher. As a professional, teaching the sons of immigrants, I tried to plant the seed of love among them. I showed them that the power is within and the American dream is still alive. All one has to do is believe! I also was able to go back to Brazil every year and visit my family: brothers, sisters, grandma and my mother.

In America I accomplished my most important goal: I became a mother of two wonderful young ladies, who became mothers on their own. Now I have three beautiful grandchildren, the most beautiful children in the whole wide world, because they are my grandchildren.

I feel deeply blessed to live in the land of the free and the brave—the United States of America, my country by choice. With gratitude I say: God bless America, the land that I love.

I hope I have loved as fully as I was able, because I believe that what will matter most when I stand face to face with my Savior is how much I loved. In the end, I believe we will all be judged by our love. Today my heart feels full—so full that there is no room for anything else.

I pray that I am living a truly Christian life, and that Christians everywhere will imitate Christ so that Christianity becomes more than a label. I believe the blood of Christ has power, and that goodness will prevail.

In God I will always trust. Forever be praised the Father, the Creator; the Son, the Redeemer; and the Holy Spirit, the creative Spirit. Thank You, Lord, for all Your gifts—especially the gift of my life. I still make mistakes because I am human, but You are divine and merciful, and in You I trust.

Papa Bill is now eighty-two and he has some health issues. I'm praying for him and doing everything possible with the help of a few doctors to slow down the disease. Unfortunately, there's no cure for dementia. I'm not looking too much into tomorrow. I'm living one day at a time and I'm enjoying it. I feel that this is the beginning of a long journey for Papa, and for me too, but we will be strong in the Lord. There are many reasons for me to become fearful, but I refuse to give into fear. My life and his life are in God's hands, and the Lord is merciful. "Jesus, in you I trust." As husband and wife, we are one body in Christ. In health or in sickness, in good times and in bad times, until death do us part. Until we meet again in the glory of God as enlightened souls.

Tonight, we are going out for dinner and later we will go to the Casino for some fun with the slot machine. Tomorrow morning we'll walk in the park and will thank the good Lord for the freshness of the morning and the song of the birds. Hand in hand we will walk until the final sunset of our lives arrives. There will be no sadness, just joy.

Photographs of My Journey

Maria riding a Lambretta (1962)

Alvinho & Maria with family before AIDS diagnosis

Alvinho, Maria, and Vovo (just before his death)

Moema — after lupus was cured through prayer and grown with Rohwan at the U of A

Family on the farm (1980s)

Most recent visit to Natal with family and friends (2025)

My Daughter Gina, Asher, Riley, and Jerry

College graduation — Bill and Maria at the University of Arizona

Our last trip to Brazil just before Bill passed (2014)

Letter to My True Loved Ones

Dear grandchildren, Rohwan, Asher and Riley,

My little ones, my beam of sunshine, I hope that when you read these words that your Vovo wrote, you can understand a little more about me, about my culture, about my life as an immigrant, as a person who made many mistakes but who wasn't afraid to say I'm sorry, and try to improve. I always tried to do better and to love more intensely. I hope that you will find something good about your Vovo "Co", your old Brazilian grandmother. Something that can make you all proud of me. I was never perfect, but I did the best I could. I know I did my best, and this makes all the difference. Now I live trusting in divine providence, hoping that I will find mercy when I arrive at the city of God because like Shakespeare said, we all are passing through, from this earth to eternity. Believe me, it's a short journey but it's a wonderful one, with its sorrows and joys.

In my youth I had so many dreams. Some of them came true, others got lost in time and in my memory. However, sometimes in a hot Tucson's summer day, with the rains from the monsoon coming down, as God's blessings to us, renewing and refreshing the desert ground, and with heavy raining clouds still hanging around in the sky, when a gentle breeze cools the city, suddenly I remember. It comes slowly into my mind, refusing to go away, bringing to this old Vovo the aroma of my unforgettable land, the aroma of jasmine of my beloved Natal, reminding me of a specific summer of my youth when I was only eighteen at the beach. I used to listen to someone saying, "You are more beautiful than this summer day!"

Now I have learned to be gentle with myself. My journey is not over yet, and I don't know how much longer I will be here. However, I will assure all of you, I am having fun. I'm enjoying the simple pleasures of life. One of my most enjoyable moments is when I have the three of you with me. You are my sunshine, looking at your little faces warms up my heart.

Rohwan, my sweetheart—what can I say to you? That I love you with all my heart? You already know that.

You have such a good heart, and it makes me so happy when you tell me, "Vovó, I love you." You are kind, smart, and strong, and the Lord has blessed you with a wonderful imagination.

You can become anything you want to be. I truly believe that. Whatever path you choose, I know you will work hard, do good, and be successful. I am so proud of you.

Asher, I love you so very much. You are a little gentleman, so sweet and gentle. It's so wonderful to see your personality developing; you are kind and considerate. You are very intelligent. I can imagine you following the steps of your father, going to Yale University to major in business, or becoming successful at any profession that you chose. I'm proud of you, my little prince. However, I know that you can choose any university in the US and any career field because whenever you choose, you will be on top.

Now you my sweet Riley, my smart little baby doll. You have leadership. I have seen you in charge many times when you play with your brother and cousin. Your Vovo loves you, too, much also. I have seen you trying to read your little books, holding them upside down, and staying at the corner of your room, for the longest time, pretending that you are reading them, showing your Vovo that you like books. Because of your love for books I can imagine you as a great writer, writing some fantastic stories, perhaps becoming a great reporter. By the way, this was one of my secret dreams, one that I couldn't realize, but who knows? It may become one of your dreams too? But only if you want to become a writer. Follow your own heart sweetheart and someday you may become the President of the United States of America. Way to go my little princess, you have the brains, you will be the best.

Follow your dreams my children, always follow your dreams, and become the person who you want to be. Each of you is a very special person, with great potential, and no matter whatever you will become in this life, I always will be proud of the three of you, just because you are you. I'm a proud grandmother, nothing that any of you could do in life is going to make me more proud because I'm already so proud of you all, just because you are you. Believe in yourselves, there is magic in believing. When you want something bad enough, remember, somehow the forces of the universe, commanded by God Almighty will conspire with you, helping you become successful. Believe in Divine Providence, it's the highest power, and with the Lord everything is possible. God has given us great inner power.

Never doubt the Lord's power. I like to repeat some thoughts from a man who I admire, a scientist named Stephen Hawking, a man who has an enormous physical disability, but also has an extraordinary mind. He once said in an interview that a goldfish sees a distorted picture of the outside world because it lives in a round bowl of water, it has a different reality than we do. We could also be in some giant goldfish bowl, and there is no unique picture of reality. The goldfish view is as valid as our own view. I like his rationale. However, this scientist's mind is relative to everything else here on this earth. Only God has the absolute mind, only God sees the true reality and for this reason you should put all your faith in the Lord. For us on this earth, everything is a mystery. I think about what we see now, we see things through a mirror. Only later we will see everything clear when we will see God face to face. Our religions tell us that we really never die, we only go into another dimension, and by faith we accept this rationale because our inner self, our soul, is eternal. Only then we will see true reality, when our souls will be united with God, the supreme being, the absolute and positive energy, the absolute love, we too will see true reality. Until then, our view of reality is no better than the reality of a goldfish inside his bowl.

Only one more thing I want to tell you all, wherever I will go, wherever I will be, I will be asking Jesus our Lord, to protect you. I will always look over the three of you. I hope someday to become an angel in heaven, a spirit of light and energy, because what your Vovo is saying it's a love promise, and God willing, I will be looking from above and protecting you all throughout your lives.

I want to tell you that on this earth, Love God above all. loved the sunrises and the sunsets, sun rises throughout your lives. Love life my sweethearts, like your Vovo did, and life will love you back. It's a wonderful gift from God.

'Now, I will give you a quote that I like. It's food for thought. For of all sad words of tongue or pen, The saddest are these: "It might have been." John G. Whittier

However, your Vovo has no regrets because the Lord knew what was best for me, and life on this earth isn't paradise for anyone. We all carry our crosses and in our pursuit of happiness we hope, but we can only be relatively happy and complete happiness we will find on the city of God, because we are created for His glory, and looking at your faces I see just that, the glorious miracle of God's love. I'm finishing the race, and now I say from my heart, it was all worth it. And finally, I leave you all with one of my favorite stanzas, "Godhead alone was hidden on the cross, but here humanity is hidden too. Believing and confessing both, I seek, What the repentant thief once sought from You."

Your forever loving, Your Vovo Co…

Maria P.S. Clark 11/26/2025

www.ingramcontent.com/pod-product-compliance
Lightning Source LLC
LaVergne TN
LVHW041542070426
835507LV00011B/881